101 VOLLEYBALL DRILLS

Peggy Martin

ISBN: 1-57167-316-4
Library of Congress Catalog Card Number: 98-87714

Cover Design: Dody Bullerman
Cover Photos: Courtesy of Central Missouri State
Developmental Editor: David Hamburg
Production Manager: Michelle A. Summers

Coaches Choice Books is a division of: Sagamore Publishing, Inc.
                                           P.O. Box 647
                                           Champaign, IL 61824-0647
                                           Web Site: http//www.sagamorepub.com

DEDICATION

This book is dedicated to my mother, Helen Martin,

and to the memory of my father, Bill Martin.

They are my heroes.

◆————————————————◆

Impact of Coaches

I have come to a frightening conclusion.
I am the decisive element in the gym or on the field.
It is my personal approach that creates the climate.
It is my daily mood that makes the weather.
As a coach, I possess tremendous power to make an athlete's life miserable or joyous.
I can be the tool of torture or an instrument of inspiration.
I can humiliate or humor, hurt or heal.
In all situations it is my response that decides whether a crisis will be escalated or de-
escalated and an athlete humanized or dehumanized.

—An adaptation of Haim Ginott—

ACKNOWLEDGMENTS

A very special thank-you to Pat Hielscher, who helped me fall in love with this game some 25 years ago.

To all the volunteer coaches in the CYO leagues of the world who did not have drill books to choose from, especially Anna Crow and Bobbie Campanaro.

To all those coaches who have shared their knowledge of the game with me, including Cecile Reynand, Debbie Brown, Mary Jo Peppler, Lisa Kissee, Lisa Love, Mick Haley, Linda Dollar, and John Kessel.

To all my colleagues, but especially Linda Delk, Lois Webb, Sandy Hoffman, Donna Palivec, Debbie Chin, and Debbie Hendricks, for the challenges and the fun.

To the world's best assistant coaches, Rhesa, Flip, and Stacy, for your continued support and loyalty. You are awesome.

To the administration at Central Missouri State University, especially Dr. Ed Elliott and Dr. Judy Vickrey, for recognizing the value of athletic participation for women, and for their support in this endeavor.

To my friends Leanna Bordner, Sheila Lillis, Cindy Smith, Joyce Bailey, and Elois Pelton, who have been so supportive throughout this project, and especially to my critical advisor, Rita Harris and my mentors Millie Barnes and Dean Martin.

Lastly, to all my former and present players who love doing these drills and who have brought so much joy to my life by playing this great game with their hearts.

CONTENTS

Chapters

PREFACE

During more than two decades of coaching, I have continually wondered how I might ever be able to give something back to the game of volleyball and to the community that supports and loves this game. It has become obvious to me that what coaches want are drills, drills, and more drills. Anytime I have had the opportunity to meet with a group of high school and/or club coaches, they have requested drills.

It is my hope that this book will provide those who are reading it with an arsenal of drills to challenge each player to improve in every aspect of the game. Toward that end, this book is a compilation of some of my favorite drills, which have been fine-tuned throughout the years.

Where do drills come from? They come from you, the volleyball community of coaches and players. Volleyball coaches are a sharing group of professionals who pass on their favorite drills so readily that the origination of these drills is seldom known. In this book, I have compiled many of those drills that have been shared with me, and I hope they will benefit your athletes as much as they have benefited mine. Occasionally, a drill will be named after the coach or player who designed that specific drill.

As the coach and leader of your team, it is your responsibility to prepare your team during practice. And what is practice but a collection of drills? Therefore, be creative; modify the design of these drills so that they best fit your team's skill level. As a vehicle for teaching and learning, properly designed drills can have great value. This book has already benefited my coaching not only because it contains all my favorite drills, but also because it categorizes them and stores them in one place.

Here's wishing you a ton of smiles as you work with this great game of volleyball and with the young athletes of today. Happy coaching!

INTRODUCTION

Coaching the sport of volleyball has always been a challenging endeavor, and it will become even more challenging in the 21st century, as athletes begin to demand more from their coaches. Tomorrow's athletes will demand that their coaches be more organized in practice situations and, therefore, more disciplined. Like today's athletes, they will insist on being entertained: Nothing less than an organized, demanding, and entertaining practice session will attract their full attention.

PURPOSE

The main purpose of this book is to assist the coach in gaining insight into drills that will challenge the volleyball player in every aspect of the game. A secondary purpose is to give the coach a working manual of organized and demanding drills from which practice sessions may be created. Another built-in purpose is to stimulate the coach to be an analyst and student of the game who chooses drills and modifies them to bring out the best performance from his or her athletes, regardless of their skill level.

SCOPE

Volleyball is a relatively young sport, and it is constantly changing, as rules are being modified yearly to enhance the game for both athlete and spectator. As a matter of fact, this work is among the first volleyball books published since the rule change at the USAV and collegiate levels, which allows players to use "finger action" when receiving served and attacked balls. As noted in several of the drills that follow, we must incorporate this new facet of the game into our existing drills.

This book begins with warm-up and conditioning drills, which are followed by a logical progression from individual skills to combination and team drills. The intent is for a coach to be able to choose a drill or two from each chapter while designing a daily or weekly practice plan. Owing to the nature of the sport of volleyball, most of the drills emphasize a combination of two or more skills. Although the only true individual skill in the game is the serve, the importance of training the setter dictates that more time be spent with the coach and the setter in one-on-one drill situations.

SOME NOTES ABOUT DRILLS

Each drill in this book is preceded by an objective, which explains what the drill is trying to do—what skills it intends for the athlete to attain. Some drills will inherently have more than one skill objective, and the coach must decide which skill to emphasize during that particular practice session. As much as possible, the drills should be game-like. The drills for warm-up in Chapter 1, for example, challenge the coach to let go of partner warm-up and partner pepper and incorporate more game-like warm-up drills.

Athletes are competitors, and the game of volleyball requires that players compete. Therefore, the more we can use competitive drills in practice, the more competitive our athletes will become. Keep in mind, however, that drill designs may have to be modified to accommodate players with varying levels of skill.

Often, conditioning will be a built-in objective of certain drills. Thus the coach must be aware that if conditioning is one of the goals of a drill, the energy and stamina it calls for will diminish the athlete's ability to execute with proper technique. (Chapter 1 suggests three separate drills for conditioning purposes only.)

Analytical coaches who are involved in practice situations will know when to scrap a drill and not beat a dead horse. They will understand that if the drill is not working, they must let it go and move on to another drill.

Leave the practice situation with a smile so everyone wants to come back for practice tomorrow. Allowing the athletes to pick the last drill of the day will give the coach an idea of their favorites. (Drill #101, The Wave, is a great end-of-practice drill.)

Attack Line: The line that extends from sideline to sideline, three meters from the net, on both sides of the court (commonly referred to as the 10-foot line).

Baseline: The line that extends from sideline to sideline, at the end of the court, on both sides of the court.

Sideline: The line that extends from baseline to baseline on both sides of the court.

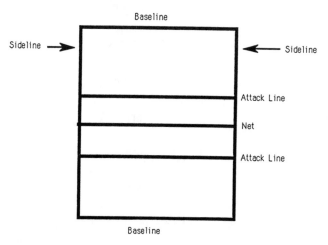

Dump: A second contact attack by any player, but usually the setter.

Down Ball: An attack ball that is hit into the opponent's court either from a distance off the net or from below the top of the net, which would be difficult to block.

Free Ball: A non-attack ball that the opponent sends over the net that should be easier to handle than a down ball.

Zones, or Areas, of the Court: The court is divided into six equal areas, starting with right back as zone 1 and continuing through zone 6 in rotational order.

Zones of the Net: The net is divided into nine zones from sideline to sideline. Zone 7 is usually the setter's zone.

C – Coach or Feeder	A – Attacker or Hitter or Spiker
B – Blocker	D – Digger or Defender or Passer
H – Hitter	LF – Left Front
S – Setter	RF – Right Front
T – Target	MF – Middle Front
P – Player or Passer	MB – Middle Blocker or Middle Front
P1 – Player 1	LB – Left Back
P2 – Player 2	RB – Right Back
P3 – Player 3	CB – Center Back
X – Player	W – Player waiting to enter drill
X1 – Player 1	Player Movement ⟶
X2 – Player 2	Ball Movement ⟿
X3 – Player 3	

WARM-UP
DRILLS

DRILL #1: THREE-PERSON PEPPER

Objective: To warm up the players; to help them improve their ball control in a game-like skill sequence.

Setup: Three players; one volleyball.

Description: Three players, spaced at least 15 feet apart, set up in a triangle. P1 tosses the ball to P3, who sets the ball back to P1, who attacks to P2, who passes (digs) to P3, who sets back to P2, who attacks to P1, who passes to P3. The setter (P3) always sets to the player who passes to her. After five contacts, players change positions. This drill does not require a net or a court.

Coaching Point: Emphasize ball control (i.e., not just batting the ball at each other) and keeping the ball continually in play.

Variation: The setter (P3) will change to the other side after every set so that both passers are passing to the right.

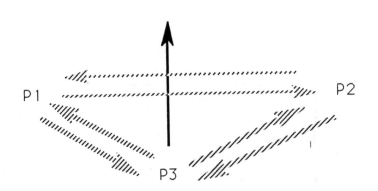

DRILL #2: THREE-PLAYERS-ON-COURT PROGRESSION

Objective: To warm up the players on the court in a game-like situation, while progressing from easy to increasingly difficult tasks.

Setup: Three players on each side of the court; one volleyball for each group.

Description: On both sides of the court, three players progress through the following steps:

- Step 1—Begin overhead passing from P1 to P2 to P3 and repeat five times before players rotate to the next position. Players should make five contacts at each position before rotating. When players return to their original position, they progress to the next step.

- Step 2—P1 makes an underhand pass to P2, who then makes an overhead pass to P3, who overhead passes back to P1. Players repeat this step five times at each position as they rotate.

- Step 3—The same as Step 2, except that P3 attacks (hits overhead) ball back to P1.

- Step 4—When the players on both courts have completed the first three steps, one side puts its ball away. The drill then continues with a down-ball attack over the net to X1, who passes to X2, who sets X3, who delivers a down ball to P1. Players repeat this step five times before rotating positions and continuing in the same manner. Both LF players transition to defense to help pass on a cross-court attack.

- Step 5—The LF players should now add a jump and off-speed attack to take the ball across the net. Again, each player should make five contacts at each position before rotating.

During each step, the players should take care never to let the ball touch the ground. If the ball does touch the ground, the player who caused the error must start over with that step of the drill. When switching positions, the players must communicate and work together on problem solving. Since the drill is being run on more than one court (although the drill will work well with only one group), both groups of players should compete to see which one finishes first. At lower skill levels, this can be a drill of endurance that can last 20-plus minutes.

Coaching Points: Do not help the players problem solve. Let them work things out on the court. Emphasize ball control, especially when the players are attacking the ball. Remind them that their shoulders should be square to the target. At lower skill levels, this drill may be completed after Step 3.

Variations: This drill can be shortened by requiring only two or three ball touches before the players change positions. This drill can also be changed to a back set, with the players attacking from RF.

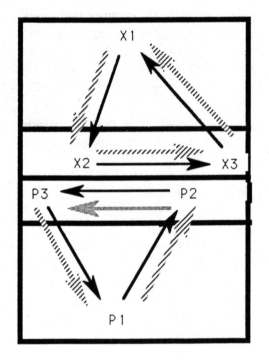

DRILL #3: GAME-LIKE WARM-UP

Objective: To have the players warm up on the court and, at the same time, improve their skills while progressing from easy to difficult tasks.

Setup: Four to six players; one volleyball per half-court.

Description: Four players take the positions of CB, S, LF, and opposing RF. The opposing RF puts the ball in play with a two-handed, overhead toss to the CB, who underhand passes to the S, who sets to the LF, who approaches and jumps—simulating an attack—and catches the set. The LF then proceeds to the opposing RF as all the other players sprint to replace the person they passed to, and the drill continues.

After two to three minutes, the RF tosser will put the ball in play by tossing it to herself and hitting the ball over to the CB. After another two to three minutes, the LF will tip the ball over the net, instead of catching it.

If more than four players are participating in the drill, those who are waiting should take positions behind the CB and the opposing RF. This drill can be done from both sides of the court without causing too much congestion.

Coaching Points: Emphasize ball control, proper approach footwork, and timing. All players should be able to execute all skills, including setting. The ball should never hit the floor.

Variation: Run the drill to the right side, utilizing a back set. When running six or more players on one half-court, put two balls in play.

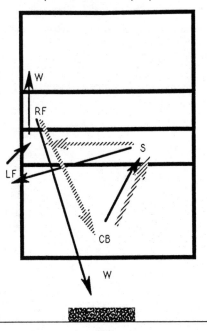

DRILL #4: SHORT, SHORT, LONG SWITCH

Objective: To improve the players' ball-handling skills during warm-up.

Setup: Three players; one volleyball.

Description: The ball begins at P1, is set to P2, and then set back to P1, who sets long to P3. As soon as P1 sets long, P1 and P2 switch places. P3 then sets to P1, who sets back to P3, who sets long to P2. P1 and P3 then switch places. This sequence should be repeated 25 times. This drill does not require a net or a court.

Coaching Points: The ball should be controlled for the entire drill and not hit the floor. Emphasize the proper overhead passing technique and footwork. Also, emphasize the importance of the players carrying over their communication from warm-up to games. In addition, require your players to call every ball that they will attempt to play.

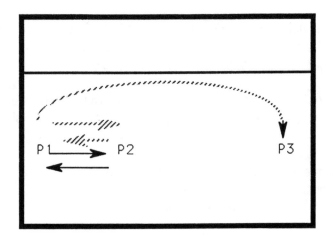

DRILL #5: TIP GAME

Objective: To help your players develop and improve their ball control while warming up in a game-like situation.

Setup: Four or eight players per court; one volleyball per half court.

Description: Place an additional antenna at mid-court on the net in order to divide the net and court in half. Set up two teams of two players each, on opposite sides of the net. Utilize the attack line as the boundary line. P1 serves from behind the attack line, and both sides play the ball out while using regular volleyball rules, except that only tips are allowed as attacks. Play a game to 11; the winner must win by two points.

Coaching Point: Require your players to communicate and to take the proper approach for their tip technique.

Variations: To speed up this drill, use rally scoring. Play a small tournament between four doubles teams, having them share the court.

P 1	P2	X3	X4
X 1	X2	P3	P4

DRILL #6: MATCH WARM-UP TEAM DEFENSE

Objective: To involve all the members of your team in a pre-match warm-up that helps prepare them by emphasizing game-like situations.

Setup: All the players on the team; a steady supply of volleyballs.

Description: During a shared-court, pre-game warm-up, the players line up at their regular defensive positions in the front and back rows, excluding a middle front. The setter takes her position at net zone 7.

The coach puts the ball in play to any backcourt player, who then passes to the setter. The setter sets either the LF or the RF, who attacks the ball back to her own defensive team. All players move back to their base positions as the ball is passed to the setter; they then move to their defensive positions while the ball is in flight and heading toward the attacker. If the ball is not set to the front-row player, that player will also assume her defensive position.

After each backcourt player digs a ball, she proceeds to the end of the line at that particular position. Each front-row player will make a designated number (in this case, five) of contacts before moving to a backcourt line and being replaced by a teammate.

Coaching Points: Remind your defensive players to be set, with their weight forward, as the attacker hits. Player movements will be dictated by the type of team defense used. (The diagrams below depict a rotation defense.)

Variations: When working with players at lower levels of skill, coaches can replace the front-row attackers. However, the players need to develop ball control when hitting the ball overhead. Add a middle hitter to simulate all possible opponent attacks.

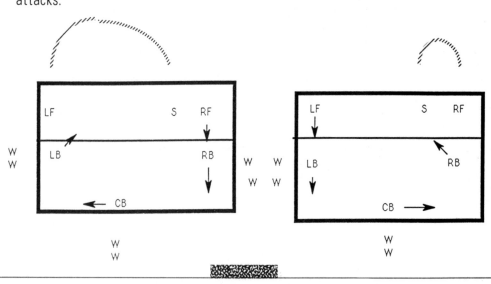

DRILL #7: GAME-LIKE HITTING

Objective: To help the players improve their hitting in pre-game or pre-practice warm-up that simulates game situations.

Setup: Six or more players; six or more volleyballs.

Description: The coach puts the ball in play across the net to a passer, while front-row players transition off the net and the setter penetrates to the net. The setter moves to the passed ball and sets any of three hitters, who then attack the ball set to them. Passers rotate after every ball that's put in play. Setters and hitters must return to defense after every attack. After 12–15 attacks, the players rotate through the drill.

Coaching Point: This is a great drill to work on the hitter's footwork off the net in transition and the setter's footwork on her release to the net.

Variations: Use opposing blockers opposite the hitters. The coach controls the difficulty of this drill through his or her method of putting the ball in play (easy to difficult).

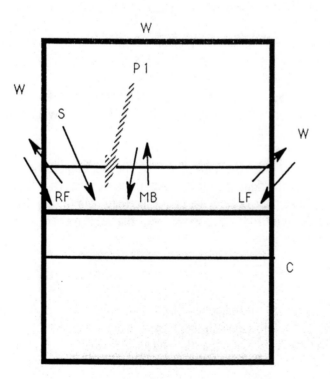

DRILL #8: CECILE'S KILLER CONDITIONING

Objective: To improve your players' conditioning by utilizing footwork, agility, quickness, and jumping skills.

Setup: Six to eight players per court; no volleyballs.

Description: Players begin at the net and execute the first five steps of this drill under the net, working from sideline to sideline. The latter steps of the drill require block jumps and attack-approach jumps. The following steps should be repeated until the players have run through them a total of three times, and as quickly as possible:

- Step 1—From under the net, and while staying low and not contacting the net, players run from the left sideline to the right sideline and sprint back along the attack line.

- Step 2—Same as Step 1, except that players face the endline and then sidestep from sideline to sideline.

- Step 3—Same as Step 2, except that players face the opposite endline.

- Step 4—Players face one sideline and move with high knees to the opposite sideline.

- Step 5—Players face one sideline and use two-foot hop (first, with feet shoulder-width apart; then, repeating, with feet together) while moving to the opposite sideline.

- Step 6—Players start at the net and assume the blocking position. Next, they take one step to the right and block-jump to the sideline. They then repeat this maneuver to the opposite sideline. (After the third time through this step, players should sprint to the opposite side of the net in preparation for the next step.)

- Step 7—Same as Step 6, except that players move to the left.

- Step 8—Players start at the net in the blocking position, then block-jump at LF, MF, and RF. (After three times through this step, players should sprint to the opposite side of the net in preparation for the next step.)

- Step 9—Same as Step 8, except players move to the left.

- Step 10—Players start at the attack line. From the LF position, they take three approach jumps and swing (same at MF, then RF), then move under the net and repeat at LF, MF, and RF.

Coaching Points: This drill provides players with a strenuous workout and can be a killer. As they tire, players will see their technique suffer; nevertheless, they should be encouraged throughout the drill to push themselves to their maximum effort.

Variation: Require the players to complete each step only once or twice, a variation that still assures a tough conditioning workout.

DRILL #9: SET OF TEN

Objective: To improve the players' conditioning.

Setup: Four to six players per half-court; no volleyballs.

Description: Players position themselves at the four corners of the court (at least one player at each corner). As quickly as possible, players block-jump at LF, then MF, then RF. Next, they turn and sprint down the right sideline, while using turn-and-go footwork and keeping their heads facing the net. At the baseline, proceeding from RB to LB, they use slide steps and sprint up the left sideline to the net. Players should repeat this maneuver 10 times and should also try to beat their teammates.

Coaching Points: Remind players about using proper technique and penetrating the net on the block, but keep in mind that fatigue will adversely affect their performance. Be sure that players do not backpedal down the right sideline.

Variation: To make this drill even more demanding, require that your players dive or roll at the deep corners of the court and/or at the intersections of the attack line and the sidelines.

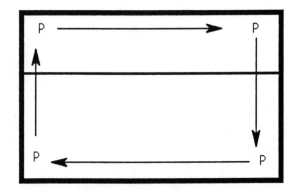

DRILL #10: CONSECUTIVE BLOCK AND APPROACH

Objective: To improve player conditioning by utilizing volleyball power moves.

Setup: At least one player; no volleyballs.

Description: Players start at their normal front-row positions at the net in a ready blocking position. They then execute a mock block jump, transition off the net utilizing a turn-and-go technique, approach, and jump with an arm swing. This maneuver should be repeated 25 times as quickly as possible. After a five-minute rest, players should do another set of 25. They should do three sets in all.

Coaching Points: Emphasize the proper footwork when releasing from the net after blocking. Allow fatigue to affect the players' power moves of jumping, but don't allow it to affect their footwork. In addition, emphasize soft landing so that the players know how to protect their legs from injury.

Variations: Place an "X" on the spot on the court that the hitter should approach from and require that she start every approach from that spot. After each block jump, have the player turn and simulate a dive-and-roll to play the ball (and have her repeat the maneuver 10 to 15 times).

SETTING
DRILLS

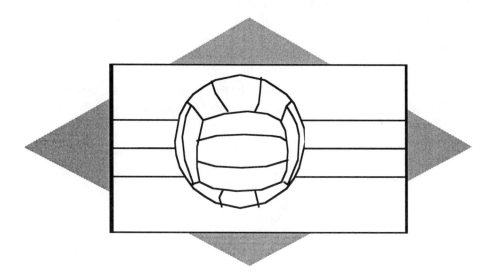

DRILL #11: SETTER WALL SERIES

Objective: To improve the players' overhead passing technique, including hand positioning and footwork.

Setup: One or more players; one volleyball per player.

Description: This drill should be done in three steps. (Each step consists of three sets of 25 repetitions.):

- Step 1—Players start by facing the wall, standing about one foot away. With the ball in their hands and above their forehead, the players set the ball one foot above their head and against the wall.

- Step 2—Players move six feet away from the wall and set the ball six feet above their head, or at antenna height, against the wall.

- Step 3—Players move 10–12 feet away from the wall and set the ball 10–12 feet above their head against the wall, allowing the ball to bounce and moving under it and setting it again.

Coaching Points: In Step 1, emphasize the proper shaping of the players' hands around the ball and the proper positioning of the ball above their forehead. In Steps 2 and 3, encourage them to use the proper footwork and to also get their hands up early.

Variation: Do not move on to Step 3 until the players have shown success in Steps 1 and 2. In Step 3, have the players set to themselves before setting to the wall.

DRILL #12: SETTER SERIES I

Objective: To improve the overhead passing technique by emphasizing the importance of the players shaping the ball with their hands and playing the ball above their forehead.

Setup: One or more players; one volleyball per player.

Description: Players start this drill on the sideline, facing the court, and proceed from sideline to sideline and back again. Each trip from one sideline to the other and back constitutes one trip. For each step below, players must complete 10 sets of 10 repetitions each, with one minute of rest between sets. Each step also requires that the players deliver two-foot-high sets to themselves:

- Step 1—Repetitive setting while walking forward.

- Step 2—Repetitive setting while walking backward.

- Step 3—Repetitive setting while sidestepping.

- Step 4—Repetitive setting while crossover stepping.

- Step 5—Repetitive setting while skipping.

Coaching Points: Focus on your players properly shaping the ball with their hands and properly positioning the ball above their forehead. Although this is listed as a setter's drill, every player should be working on her overhead passing skills.

Variations: Instruct your players to increase the height of their sets to six to 10 feet above their head. Decrease the number of sets.

DRILL #13: SETTER SERIES II

Objective: To improve the overhead passing technique, including hand positioning and footwork.

Setup: One or more players; one volleyball per player.

Description: Players start this drill on the sideline, facing the court. They then complete the following steps, doing 10 sets of 10 repetitions and resting for one minute between sets:

- Step 1—Jump-set to self.

- Step 2—Set to ceiling, allowing the ball to bounce before setting again.

- Step 3—Same as Step 2, but add a 180-degree turn after each set.

- Step 4—Same as Step 2, but touch the floor between sets.

- Step 5—Same as Step 2, but add a 180-degree turn and back set.

Coaching Points: Emphasize the importance of footwork, so that the players are able to get under each set with a left-right technique. Also, instruct the players to get their hands up early.

Variations: Have your players employ other actions between sets, such as a sit-down, a dive, or a roll.

DRILL #14: SETTER CATCH AND TOSS

Objective: To improve the overhead passing technique, including hand positioning and footwork.

Setup: Two players; one volleyball.

Description: Players begin the drill by facing each other from a distance of about 10 feet. Players toss and catch the ball above their forehead, simulating the setting action from their footwork to the ball to their follow-through after release. After 25 repetitions, the players should rest, then repeat.

Coaching Points: This is an excellent drill for beginning setters and other players. It is also a good drill for the experienced player who wants to review the proper overhead passing techniques. Do not allow players to actually set the ball until every catch and toss is accomplished by using the proper technique.

Variations: Increase the distance between the players. Instead of tossing the ball directly to her partner, each player should try tossing it away so that her partner has to move right, and then left, two steps. She should also alternate short and long tosses.

DRILL #15: SET CLOSE/SET FAR

Objective: To improve consistency in setting over a variety of distances.

Setup: Two players; one volleyball.

Description: Players start the drill by facing each other, with one player (P1) on the baseline and the other (P2) on the attack line. P1 sets the ball antenna height to P2 and immediately moves to about the 20-foot line and asks for a "near" set return. P2 returns the set to P1, who then sets back to P2 and retreats to the baseline and asks for a "far" set. After 25 repetitions, the players change positions and then repeat the drill.

Coaching Points: This drill calls for your players to communicate on each set. Require the retreating player to "turn and go" and not backpedal.

Variations: Increase the distance and height of the sets. To make the drill more game-like for setters, place them at the net, with P1 at the LF sideline and P2 in Zone 7. The drill above is more of an overhead passing drill than a setting drill.

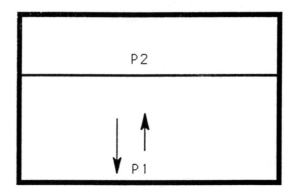

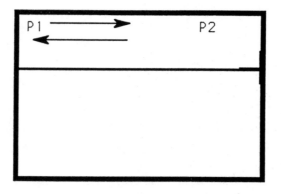

DRILL #16: PARTNER-SETTING SERIES

Objective: To practice ball control and footwork while overhead passing.

Setup: Two players; one volleyball.

Description: Players begin the drill by facing each other from a distance of 15–20 feet. Each of the following steps should be done for two to three minutes, before the players progress to the next step. Players should set to their partners 10–15 feet above their head.

- Step 1—Set to yourself five feet above your head, then set to your partner, who does the same.

- Step 2—Set to yourself, turn 180 degrees, set to yourself again, turn another 180 degrees, then set your partner, who does the same.

- Step 3—Repeat Step 1, but with 90-degree turns.

- Step 4—Set to your partner, then squat and touch the floor.

- Step 5—Set to your partner, side-step two steps to your right and left, and then move back to your starting position before the next contact.

- Step 6—Set to your partner, do a roll, and then step back to your starting position.

Coaching Points: The players will become fatigued and, as a result, their technique will suffer. Hence, the goal of this drill can be enhanced conditioning or improved technique, but not both (at least not equally).

Variation: Choose three of the six steps daily, instead of all six at one time.

DRILL #17: THREE-SETTER FIGURE EIGHT

Objective: To improve setting consistency while moving.

Setup: Three players; one volleyball.

Description: Players begin this drill by facing each other from a distance of 15 feet (see diagram below for clarification). P1 runs the figure eight while P2 and P3 remain stationary. P1 sets to P2 and follows the set by running around P2. P2 sets to P3, who returns the set to P1, who sets P3 and follows the set by running around P3. After 25 repetitions, P1 replaces P2, who becomes the runner.

This drill should be run enough times so that all three players run the figure eight. This drill need not be done on a court.

Coaching Points: Emphasize the importance of your players getting to the ball quickly and getting their hands up early. Require that the players call every ball.

DRILL #18: THREE-SETTER BACK SETTING

Objective: To improve consistency in setting and back setting from various distances.

Setup: Three players; one volleyball.

Description: Players begin the drill by standing in a line, about 10 feet from each other. P1 sets the ball to P2, who sets to P3, who back-sets to P1. (After every back set, P3 turns 180 degrees to her right.) P1 sets to P2, who sets back to P1, who sets to P3, who back-sets to P2. After 25 back sets, the players rotate. This drill need not be done on a court.

Variation: Instruct your players to set the ball to themselves once (five feet high) before setting to another player.

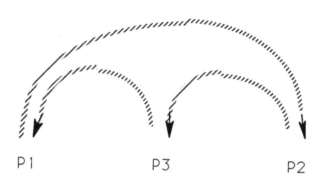

P1   P3   P2

DRILL #19: ONE FOOT UP

Objective: To help setters develop the proper footwork when they are releasing to the net and coming off the net.

Setup: One to three players; no volleyballs.

Description: This drill begins with setters in the RB defensive position. On the coach's signal, the setters release to the net. Upon reaching net zone 7, the setters lift their left foot and wait for the coach's command. Once they get the coach's signal, the setters take three steps away from the net and toward the 10-meter line, then square themselves to LF and begin simulating the setting action. The setters then move to cover at LF, before returning to the RB defensive position. Setters repeat this drill 25 times. (See Diagram A below for the setters' movement.)

Coaching Points: Allow your setters to develop efficient footwork while getting to the net and also while moving off the net to set.

Variations: Require the setters to practice their footwork from every serve receive position (Diagram B below), as well as from the defensive position. The coach should try tossing the ball and having the setters catch the ball and freeze, allowing the coach to check their body alignment toward the target.

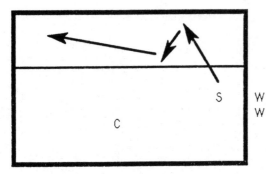

Diagram A

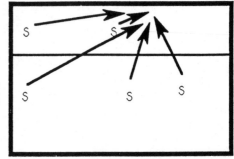

Diagram B

DRILL #20: BOUNCE TO SET

Objective: To train the back-row setter to use an efficient movement to the net and to practice setting in a game-like transition.

Setup: One or two players; steady supply of volleyballs.

Description: The setter starts the drill at the RB position. As the coach bounces the ball, the setter releases to the net and sets the bounced ball to LF and then follows her set to her cover position. The setter then proceeds to her defensive position as the coach bounces another ball. The bounced ball will be much like a dig from the backcourt. The setter should set 50 balls, then rest and repeat.

Coaching Points: Emphasize the proper footwork to the ball, as well as the proper weight transfer at the point of contact. Run the drill quickly with two setters.

Variations: The coach can move to different areas of the backcourt so that every possible digging angle is replicated. Require the setters to back-set and/or alternate sets to LF and RF.

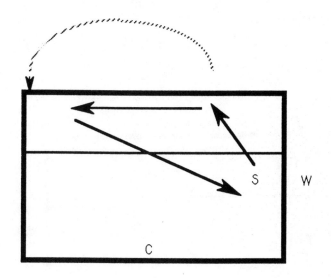

DRILL #21: TARGET SETTING

Objective: To train the setter to consistently set to a target from various positions at the net.

Setup: One player; one volleyball.

Description: The setter is positioned in net zone 7, while the coach stands on a box at net zone 1.

The coach begins the drill by tossing the ball to the setter, who returns the set to the coach (50 repetitions). The coach then alternates between tossing balls close—so the setter must move toward net zone 1 to set—and far away—so the setter must set from a distance (50 repetitions). The coach then alternates tosses off the net and on the net (50 repetitions).

Coaching Points: Give the setter feedback on every set. Make corrections so that you help the setter become consistent. Boxes (like the one the coach is standing on) are used in target-setting drills so that the target can reach and catch the ball at the height the hitter would hit the ball, and also so that the setter and coach can evaluate the setter's consistency.

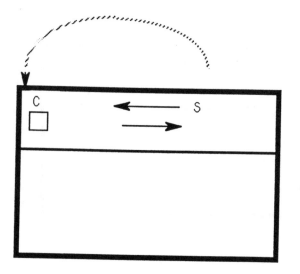

DRILL #22: TRIANGLE SETTING TO TARGET

Objective: To train the setter to consistently set to a target from net zone 7.

Setup: One player; steady supply of volleyballs.

Description: With the setter positioned in net zone 7, the coach begins the drill by tossing the ball from the backcourt. The setter then sets to the target, who is standing on a box at LF. The coach controls and varies the types of passes made to the setter from perfect passes to bad passes. The setter sets 50–75 balls, then rests and repeats the drill.

Coaching Points: Emphasize the need for the setter to consistently place the ball two to three feet off the net to the LF target. The target should give feedback to the setter on every set.

Variations: Add a box and a target at RF and/or MF and have the setter alternate setting to each position.

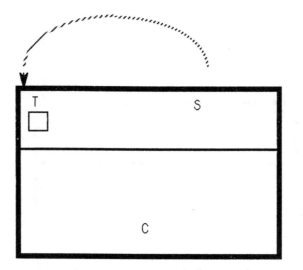

DRILL #23: TARGET-SETTING TWO DIFFERENT SETS

Objective: To train the setter to consistently and effectively deliver a variety of sets to her targets.

Setup: One player; steady supply of volleyballs.

Description: The setter, positioned in net zone 7, sets tossed balls from the coach, alternating her sets to LF and MF targets, who are standing on boxes. The coach controls and varies the types of passes to the setter, alternating perfect passes and bad passes. The setter sets 50–75 balls, then rests and repeats the drill.

Coaching Points: Make the drill easy to difficult by tossing perfect to bad passes. Emphasize consistency to the setter, encouraging her to strive for a goal of 40 perfect sets in 50 attempts.

Variation: Add a target on a box at RF and/or at the three-meter line for backcourt attack sets. Require the setter to penetrate from the RB position before every set.

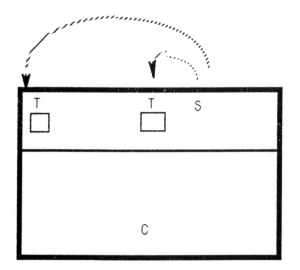

DRILL #24: SETTER TRAINING WITH VERBAL CUES

Objective: To train the setter to use the same body mechanics for every ball she sets by utilizing verbal cues.

Setup: One player; steady supply of volleyballs.

Description: The setter in net zone 7 sets tossed balls from her coach. As each tossed ball approaches the setter, the coach will call out the specific set to be delivered (e.g., out, middle, back, or something more specific). The setter will set 50–75 balls, then rest and repeat the drill.

Coaching Points: Emphasize to the setter the importance of setting every ball with the same body alignment so that blockers will have a difficult time anticipating where the set might go. When your players have reached a higher skill level, have the setters jump-set every ball.

Variation: Add a MB on the opposite side of the net, who will attempt to "read" the setter. The MB should take one step in the direction of the anticipated set, a move that will give the setter feedback as to whether she is fooling the MB.

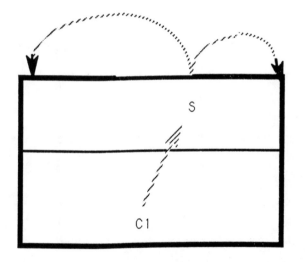

DRILL #25: SETTER TRAINING WITH HAND SIGNALS

Objective: To train the setter to look away from the volleyball and still be able to deliver a good set.

Setup: One player; steady supply of volleyballs.

Description: The setter in net zone 7 will set tossed balls from the coach (C1). A second coach (C2), who is standing at the opposing MF, signals to the setter (signaling with hand held at waist) which set to deliver. The setter must look away from the ball in order to see the signal. The signal can be basic (e.g., pointing out or back) or more specific (e.g., using a numbered setting system).

Coaching Points: This drill is an advanced setter training drill that forces the setter to look at the opponent's MB.

Variation: Have C2 give signals from the attack line in front of the setter. This method forces the setter to look away from the ball to her own court. It is also an easier drill than the one above.

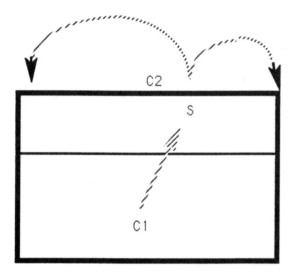

DRILL #26: SETTER VS. MB

Objective: To train the setter to decide whether to set front or back, depending on the movement of the MB.

Setup: Two players; steady supply of volleyballs.

Description: The setter in net zone 7 sets tossed balls from the coach, with her set selection based on the movement of the opposing MB. As the tossed ball approaches the setter, the opposing MB takes a big step left or right. The setter then chooses to set LF or RF, depending on the movement of the blocker and the blocker's commitment to one direction or the other. The setter sets in the opposite direction of the blocker's movement.

Coaching Points: In order to achieve the proper timing called for in this drill, the coach may find it necessary to act as the opposing MB.

Variation: The setter penetrates from the RB position and/or all the serve receive positions. Require the setter to jump-set all balls.

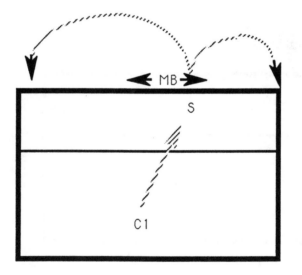

DRILL #27: SETTER ONE-ON-ONE

Objective: To train the front-row setter to know when to set or attack, depending on the blocker's commitment.

Setup: Two players; steady supply of volleyballs.

Description: The setter in net zone 7 jump-sets or dumps/hits tossed balls from the coach, and bases her set selection on the movement of the opposing LF blocker. The setter chooses to either set LF or MF or attack, depending on whether the LF jumps with the setter or stays down.

Coaching Points: Instruct the LF blocker to commit as she would during a game situation so that the drill is game-like for the setter.

Variation: The setter penetrates from the RB position and/or all serve receive positions.

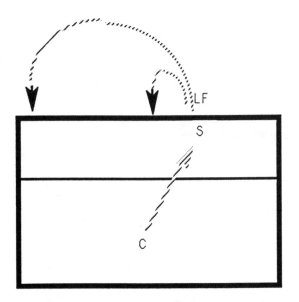

DRILL #28: SAVE THE ATTACK

Objective: To train the setter to retrieve all bad passes and convert them into balls that can be attacked; to turn balls that are passed into the net into balls that can be set.

Setup: One player; steady supply of volleyballs.

Description: The coach begins this drill by tossing balls to the setter in net zone 7, making sure that she tosses them at varying speeds and heights so as to simulate errant passes into the net. The setter attempts to retrieve each ball out of the net with a bump set to either the outside hitter or the backcourt attacker.

Coaching Points: Instruct the setter to attempt to turn every pass into a ball that can be hit, regardless of how bad the pass might be. Setters must practice retrieving every possible errant pass, including balls that are passed high into the net, low into the net, hard into the net, and soft into the net. Do not let setters be satisfied just getting the ball out of the net; the goal must be to attack.

Variations: The setter penetrates from the RB position. The coach tosses balls that the setter attempts to intercept before they go into the net; the coach then forces the setter to make more decisions by mixing in bad passes (high, low, soft, hard). Add LF hitter to the attack so the setter can evaluate her ability to save the attack.

DRILL #29: SETTER AND ONE HITTER

Objective: To train the setter to deliver her sets accurately to one hitter.

Setup: Four players; steady supply of volleyballs.

Description: Handling the coach's tosses, the setter in zone 7 sets or jump-sets one hitter at each of the hitting positions. Each hitter communicates with the setter as the coach tosses the ball to the setter. Each hitter will take six swings.

Coaching Points: Instruct the hitters to communicate on every tossed ball so as to let the setter know which set to deliver. Either let the hitters create their own sequence, or assume responsibility and take control over which sets each hitter should take. The setter's goal is to deliver accurate sets to each hitter so that every ball is hit into the court without contacting the net.

Variation: Add a passer to make the drill more game-like.

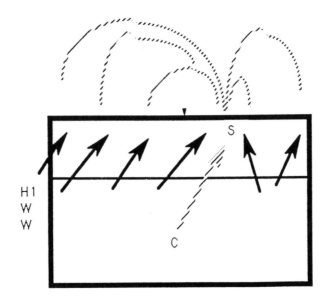

DRILL #30: SETTER AND TWO HITTERS

Objective: To train the setter to deliver sets accurately to two hitters.

Setup: Five to seven players; steady supply of volleyballs.

Description: Receiving the coach's tosses, the setter in net zone 7 sets or jump-sets two hitters, one at the MF hitting position and the other at either LF or RF. The MF hitter calls and approaches for a quick set as the coach tosses the ball to the setter. The setter delivers three sets to each hitter before two new hitters replace the two original hitters.

Coaching Points: Instruct your hitters to communicate on every tossed ball so they can let the setter know which set to deliver. Either let the hitters create their own sequence, or assume responsibility and take control over which sets each hitter should take. This drill is more game-like in that the setter has the MF hitter up and in her vision on every pass, and she must manage not to get distracted, yet, at the same time, be able to set the outside hitter accurately.

Variation: Add a passer and blockers and have the setter release and return to the RB defensive position after every set.

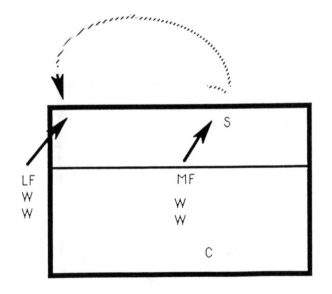

DRILL #31: QUICKS VS. ONE BLOCKER

Objective: To train the setter to deliver quick sets to the hitter so that the hitter can consistently beat one blocker.

Setup: Three to five players; steady supply of volleyballs.

Description: The setter in net zone 7 takes the coach's toss and then sets or jump-sets quicks to the MH. The opposing MB, meanwhile, attempts to block the quick hitter. She does this by stepping either left or right as the MH approaches, thus taking away one of the hitter's angles. It is the setter's job to read the blocker and deliver the set so that the hitter hits past the blocker to the angle the blocker leaves open.

In this drill, either one hitter should hit 10 in a row, or all the middles should take turns hitting and also periodically switch off with the blocker.

Coaching Points: Instruct the setter to deliver the ball directly above her head so she will force the hitter to hit to the opponent's LB. If the blocker commits to take away the shot to LB, instruct the setter to set the ball past the hitter's right shoulder, and closer to her left shoulder, to force the hitter to hit to the opponent's RB.

Variation: Require that the setter penetrate from the RB position.

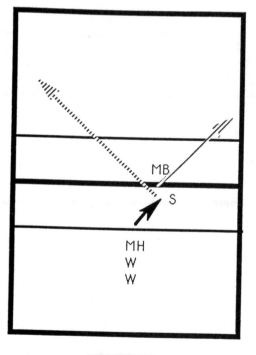

DRILL #32: COMBOS VS. ONE BLOCKER

Objective: To train the setter to deliver sets to combo hitters, depending on the MB's commitment to one or the other hitter.

Setup: Six to eight players; steady supply of volleyballs.

Description: The setter in net zone 7 takes the coach's toss and either sets or jump-sets a quick middle attack or the second-option attack to the crossing hitter. The opposing MB then attempts to block either the quick hitter or the second-option hitter. As the MH approaches, the MB will commit to either of the hitters, so it is the setter's job to read the blocker and deliver the set to the open hitter. In this drill, each pair of hitters runs six combo plays before being replaced by two new hitters.

Coaching Points: Give the setter feedback when she makes correct decisions.

Variation: Require that the setter penetrate from the RB defensive position. Utilize this drill to practice all combo plays.

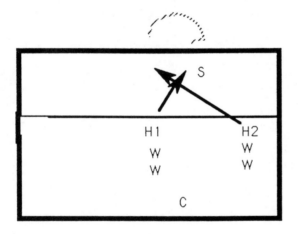

DRILL #33: BLOCK AND DECIDE

Objective: To improve the front-row setter's decision making; to practice executing jump-sets, dumps, attacks, and blocks after the initial block.

Setup: One to three setters (or RF players); steady supply of volleyballs.

Description: The setter, or RF player, mock blocks and turns immediately to receive a tight dig (toss) from the coach. The In this drill, the setter must decide to either jump-set, dump, attack, or block, without a net foul. After the setter begins making consistently good decisions and executing the correct technique, the coach should add an opposing LF blocker to the scenario. The blocker's commitment will affect the setter's decision making.

Coaching Points: Front-row setters should be able to get every tight ball in play without committing net fouls. Encourage them to react quickly to an overpass to block the opponent's attack.

Variation: Add a RB passer, who will either dig the ball to the setter off of the coach's tip or attack over the net.

DRILL #34: "D" FOR SETTERS

Objective: To help the setter practice and learn to release and defend on attacks from the opponent's RF; to foster communication between right-side front-row and back-row players.

Setup: Two players; steady supply of volleyballs.

Description: The RF and RB take their base defensive positions. On the coach's command, they move into position to prepare for the opponent's RF attack. (Note: These two players should switch positions after every 10 attacks.) The coach hits or tips the ball to the right side. If the back-row setter digs the ball, then the RF sets to the target. If the RF non-setter digs the ball, then the RB setter moves in to set to either the target or back to the RF, who then transitions to offense after digging.

Coaching Points: Communication between the two players is mandatory. The RF may attack the second ball.

Variation: Allow both players to set the target at the MF position.

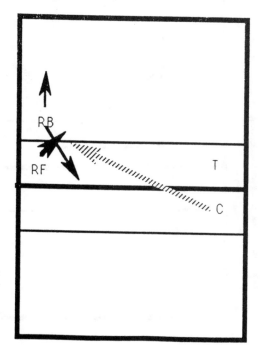 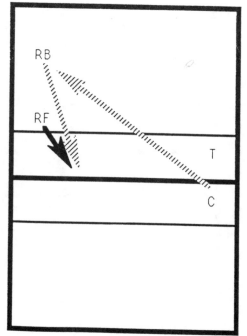

DRILL #35: SETTER TRANSITION

Objective: To help the setter practice and learn exactly what to do in a game, including setting, defense, coverage, and communication.

Setup: Three to four players; 10–12 balls.

Description: (1) The coach hits the ball to the setter in RB, who digs to the target; (2) the coach slaps the ball for a free ball, and the setter releases; (3) the coach hits or tosses the ball to the passer, who passes to the setter; (4) the setter sets, covers, and returns to her defensive position, and the drill starts again.

Coaching Point: Emphasize to the setter the importance of releasing as soon as she sees that the ball is not directed to RB.

Variations: Add a LF attacker, who will hit the set ball. Change the pattern of the drill to be more game-like and unpredictable (e.g., hit two consecutive balls to the setter and three to the passer).

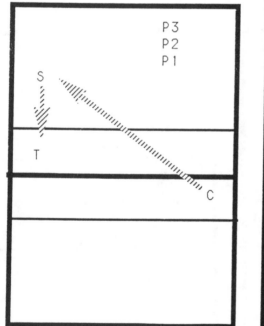 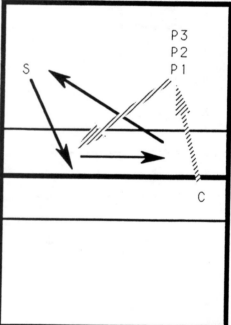

SERVE AND SERVE-RECEIVE DRILLS

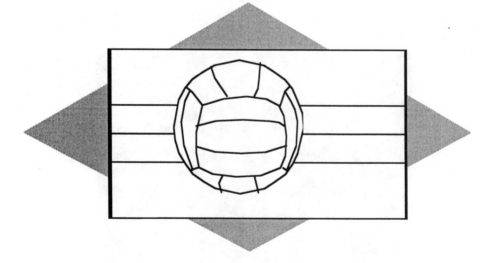

DRILL #36: MISS THE TARGET SERVING

Objective: To improve the servers' accuracy and placement by having her practice serving to unoccupied areas of the opponent's court.

Setup: Two to six players; one volleyball for every two servers; targets on both sides of the court (i.e., cones, chairs, towels, or people) that are stationed in the opponent's serve receive formation.

Description: Servers work with partners and attempt to miss the targets while serving. In this scenario, one partner serves, while the partner opposite retrieves the ball and returns the serve. The coach should set goals according to the players' skill level (e.g., 20 consecutive target misses, 10 good serves, 10 serves to each open area).

Coaching Points: More often than not, drills that carry over to games require players to serve to a target. This drill is an exception, however, because it emphasizes serving away from opponents. Tough serving should be a high priority for every team, especially with the advent of the rule that OKs finger action when receiving the serve.

Variations: In order to increase the difficulty of the drill, add some nuances from the other drills in this chapter, such as "serving under the elastic" or sprinting onto the court and assuming a defensive position after each serve.

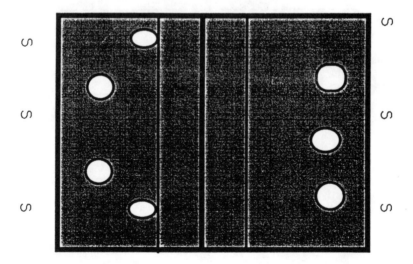

DRILL #37: BEAT COACH

Objective: To help the servers become accustomed to game-like pressure when serving, by including a consequence (i.e., a penalty for an errant serve) and emphasizing accuracy and serve placement.

Setup: 1–12 players; steady supply of volleyballs.

Description: The coach should set up two serving lines of equal numbers of players and give each player a ball. The drill begins with the first player serving a game to 15 points. For any serve that is an error, the coach gets 2–5 points. Each server must beat the coach before completing the drill.

Coaching Points: Emphasize concentration. Decide how to score on the basis of the skill level of your servers or the amount of pressure placed on them. Five points for the coach on every missed serve by the server would give the game to the coach after three such misses.

Variation: Require servers to serve to certain zones of the court in order to score.

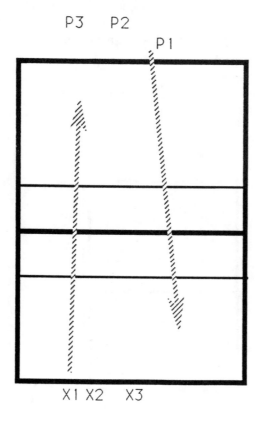

DRILL #38: GOLF

Objective: To help servers improve their placement prior to sprinting to defense; to help them enhance their conditioning.

Setup: 6–12 players; 6–12 volleyballs (1 per player).

Description: The coach sets up two serving lines of equal numbers of players. Each player has a ball. The first player in each line attempts to serve to "hole" (or area) No. 1. If the ball hits in the immediate area, then the server gets one point. The server then sprints to her defensive position, touches the floor, and continues sprinting to retrieve a served ball and to get in the opposite serving line. The next players in line repeat the maneuver.

After an attempt is made to serve to all the holes, the game is over. This drill can be run on two courts to accommodate the entire team, or on one court only with six servers.

Coaching Points: Either the coach or the players may keep score. Keep track of which holes are the most difficult for the players to score on and reteach the proper technique for serving to that particular area. This is a competitive drill that your players will like. Play nine holes every day and tabulate the scores to figure out your weekly winner.

Variations: Require servers to serve two or three balls at each hole, so that they have more opportunity for practice, or simply have them play 18 holes instead of nine.

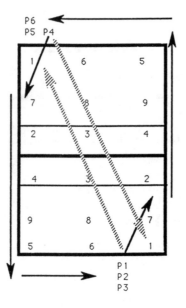

DRILL #39: SERVE OR DIE

Objective: To help servers practice serving while they are fatigued.

Setup: 6–12 players; 6–12 volleyballs.

Description: Run a strip of elastic from one antenna to the other, approximately eight inches from the top, making sure the elastic is tautly attached to the antennae. Set up two teams of equal numbers of players at the serving line. Each player in line, except the first player, has a ball.

The drill begins as the first player in each line sprints from the baseline to the attack line and back four times, and then serves the ball. P2 starts her sprints as P1 finishes her second. Each team scores 1 point for each serve under or contacting the elastic; 0 points for a good serve over the elastic; and minus-1 point for an error. The first team to 11 or 15 wins.

Coaching Points: This drill is much more game-like, because it has a built-in fatigue factor: Players must focus on serving after sprinting, leaving them fatigued in much the same way they are after a long rally.

Variations: Require servers to serve to certain zones for bonus points. At beginning skill levels, the elastic should not be utilized and the drill run to get serves "over and in."

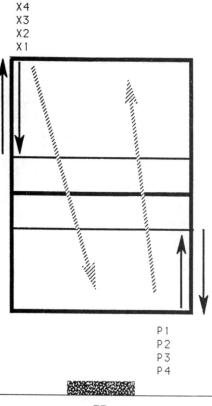

DRILL #40: ACE TO REPLACE

Objective: To help the players learn how to serve and pass tough serves.

Setup: Six to eight players; steady supply of volleyballs.

Description: On one side of the court, the coach sets up as many passers as used in team serve-receive formation with a target. On the other side, the coach sets up a serving line. In this drill, servers will attempt to "ace" the passers. If the servers succeed, they then take the place of the passers who were aced. The passers' goal is to stay on the receiving side for the entire drill, or as long as possible. Passers rotate after every five serves.

Coaching Points: Emphasize aggressive serving, at least within limits. Keep in mind that if, for example, every other serve is an error, then the passers will not get any practice opportunities. By the same token, however, passers do need to practice recognizing "out" serves.

Variations: Define an ace as any pass that the target can neither catch nor set, or any pass for which the target must take more than one step to set. Use a setter at the target position to set every ball.

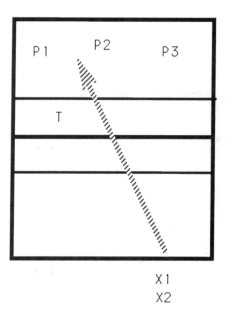

DRILL #41: SERVE AND RUN

Objective: To help servers learn to make tough serves away from the middle of the court.

Setup: Eight players; four volleyballs.

Description: On both sides of the court, the coach sets up two targets, or players, who will score serves, and also a serving line.

In this drill, the servers attempt to serve deep and to the sidelines outside the targets. After each serve, the servers will chase the ball and get in the other serving line. The goal is for each server to score 21 points in a three-minute period. The targets will score each serve for the server by signaling the server with their fingers. The servers will tally their own score. Servers get minus-1 point for each error; 0 points for balls served between targets to the middle of the court; 2 points for balls served outside the targets, but short; and 3 points for balls served deep and past targets. Servers become targets after three minutes.

Coaching Point: Emphasize aggressive serving.

Variations: Vary the locations of the targets, and also vary the point scoring, depending on whether you wish to make the drill easier or more difficult.

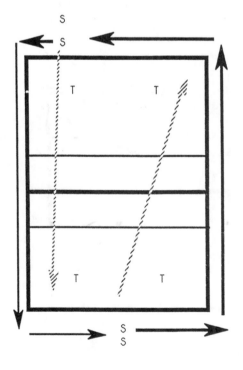

DRILL #42: FIFTEEN-POINT GAME

Objective: To help your players serve and receive in fast-paced situations.

Setup: 12 players; steady supply of volleyballs.

Description: On one side of the court, set up three passers; keep two other passers waiting. All other players should be in a serving line on the opposite side of the court, and the first player in line begins the drill by serving.

After every serve, the passers move one position to their right. The coach determines whether the passer receives a point for a perfect pass. If so, the player who is credited with the point calls out her current score. If the passer is aced, however, she joins the serving line, and the server joins the passing line. An ace counts as a point for the server, and she calls out her current score. When the coach considers a pass "just OK," no one scores and no one is replaced. The first player to 15 points wins.

Coaching Point: To encourage a high percentage of good serves, penalize players who miss their serves by requiring them to run sprints or do push-ups before they can rejoin the drill.

Variations: Define an ace as any pass that the target cannot catch or set, or any pass for which the target must take more than one step to set. Also, try using the setter as the target.

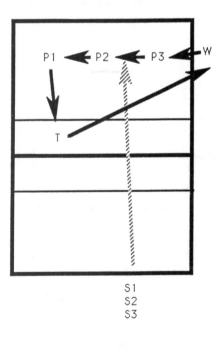

DRILL #43: TWENTY-ONE–POINT TEAM PASSING

Objective: To help your players learn how to control their serves and passes; to build teamwork.

Setup: Entire team; six volleyballs.

Description: The coach divides the team evenly, setting up one passing line, one serving line, and one target line on each side of the court.

The drill begins as the first server on one side serves to the passer on the opposite side, who passes to the target. The server then moves to the passing line on her own side of the court. After passing, the passer moves to the target line on the same side of the court. The target, meantime, proceeds to the serving line on the same side of the court as well. The object of this drill is for the entire team to become involved in working toward 21 points (as scored out loud by the coach). Every pass that the target can catch in net zone 7 scores 1 point; balls that the target can catch out of net zone 7 score 0 points; and shanks that hit the floor before the target can make the catch are minus-1 point. The coach keeps the cumulative score until the team reaches 21.

Coaching Points: In this drill, the servers are attempting to control their serve to a certain passer or area of the court. Emphasize passing form. This is also an excellent drill for working on receiving the serve with the overhead pass.

Variation: The coach designates which area the passers pass from and which area the servers serve from (e.g., servers serve from area 1 to area 1 on one half of the court, while servers serve from area 5 to area 5 on the other half).

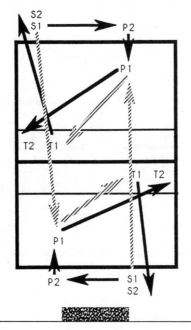

DRILL #44: PERPETUAL SERVE RECEIVE

Objective: To help your players improve their serving and receiving by practicing those skills in a perpetual-movement, game-like drill.

Setup: Six or more players; steady supply of volleyballs.

Description: The coach sets up each side of the court with three passers on the court and one waiting; two servers; and two targets. The first server begins the drill by serving and then sprinting to the opposite side of the court to the waiting-passer position. Next, the first passer passes to a target and becomes a target.

The targets, meanwhile, become servers on their own side of the court. If the server misses her serve, she gets another ball and serves again after the next server. This drill can be timed, or it can also be stopped after a certain number of passes to the target.

Coaching Points: Servers in this drill are attempting to control their serve to a certain passer or area of the court, so emphasize serve control rather than maximum toughness. This would be a good drill in which to incorporate practice receiving serves with the overhead pass.

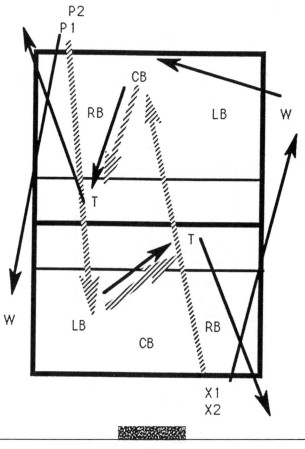

DRILL #45: SERVE VS. PASS FOR POINTS

Objective: To help your players with their serve receive and serving by putting game-like pressure on them.

Setup: 12 players; steady supply of volleyballs.

Description: Divide the players into teams of six, with one team acting as the receiving team and the other acting as the serving team. (After 18 serves, the teams will reverse their roles.)

The drill begins with the servers serving 18 balls and alternating after every serve. Points are awarded thus: 5 points to the serving team for an ace; minus-5 points for a serving error; 0 points if the receiving team keeps serves in play. The receiving team passes from team serve-receive patterns and rotates after every serve. The scoring for the passing (receiving) team is done on a 3-point scale: 3 points for a perfect pass; 2 points for giving the setter two options; 1 point for giving the setter only one option; 0 points for an overpass; and minus-1 point for a reception error.

Coaching Points: The point system rewards servers for attempting to serve aggressively. The two teams compete for the highest total points.

Variation: Require the teams to play to 15 or 21 points before switching assignments.

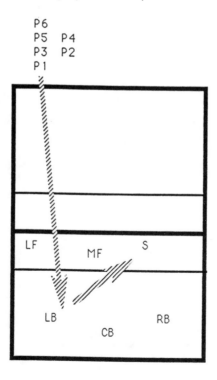

PASSING AND DIGGING DRILLS

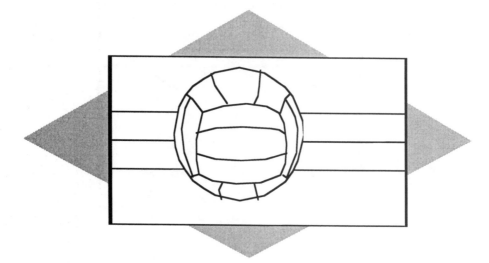

DRILL #46: TWO-PLUS-TWO EXCHANGE

Objective: To help improve your players' free-ball passing while working with a teammate and communicating on every pass.

Setup: Four players; steady supply of volleyballs.

Description: Stationed on the same half of the court, two teams of two players pass balls tossed from the coach to the target. After every team contact, players switch places. Players must communicate on each pass and switch. The coach, meantime, fires balls rapidly and randomly at both teams.

This drill can be timed, or the target can keep score for each team. Score 1 point for every pass to the target, minus-1 point for passes made without switching. The winner is the first team to reach 25 points.

Coaching Points: Allow the players to problem-solve when deciding how to make their position switch; give only minimal instruction. Keep in mind that all free-ball passes should be perfect passes to the target at antenna height. Also, ball shaggers are essential to the smooth running of this drill.

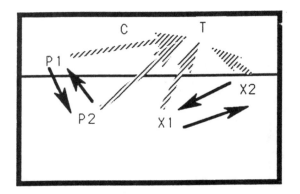

DRILL #47: KELLY'S ASTER

Objective: To practice running to and through the ball when free-ball passing.

Setup: Four players per half-court; three volleyballs.

Description: On one side of the court, set up four players, with two of the players actually going through the drill and the other two running the drill. P1 and P2 will run through the drill three times before switching with P3 and P4.

P1 starts at deep LB and begins the drill by running through the tossed ball from P3 and passing to the target. P1 then quickly runs to area 1, where P3 has tossed another ball, which P1 passes to the target. Another ball is tossed to area 2, where P1 again passes to the target before sprinting back to LB. P2 begins the drill as soon as P1 has completed her third pass.

After three times through the drill, the passers switch places with the tosser and the target, and the drill is repeated.

Coaching Points: This is a player-run drill. However, at lower skill levels, the coach should be the tosser in order to ensure that the drill is run at the proper pace. Also, emphasize that every pass should be of antenna height.

Variation: To speed up the drill, use two tossers, with two passers moving through the drill at the same time.

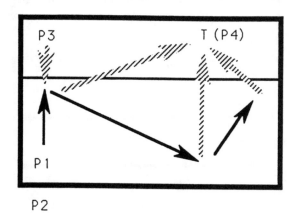

DRILL #48: SEAN'S FREEZE THREES

Objective: To force players to focus on their platform and ball control on defense in a competitive situation.

Setup: 6–8 players; 10 volleyballs.

Description: On both sides of the court, set up four players, with three in the backcourt and a setter at the net.

The coach initiates the drill by hitting a ball across the net to the three deep defenders. The player digging the ball must freeze her platform and look at it after contact with the ball, counting "one thousand and one." The ball is played out in 4-on-4, with only backcourt attacking allowed. Each first contact in the rally requires that player to follow the "freeze" rule, and the rally ends immediately if the player does not freeze properly. The next rally is initiated by the coach, who involves the team on the other side of the court.

Teams should play out the game using rally scoring, making sure to switch sides after eight points are scored, so that each team faces the coach as both a right-side and left-side attacker.

Variations: Set up the drill 3-on-3 without the setters. Also, have the players in the backcourt play their normal defensive position, or have them rotate after every rally.

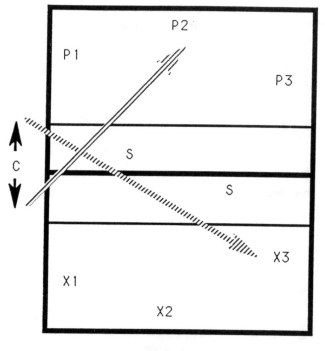

DRILL #49: DIGGING AROUND THE WORLD

Objective: To teach the players how to dig to the target from all angles of the court.

Setup: Four players; steady supply of volleyballs.

Description: In this drill, P1 will dig balls to the setter from eight positions on the court, beginning at the attack line at LF.

The coach attacks from atop a box across the net to each position (1–8). The coach's attack to position 8 will be a tip that the player must touch before exiting that portion of the drill. Meanwhile, the other players will act as targets in the setter's zone, as well as ball shaggers, before they begin rotating into the drill. Score is kept by awarding a point for every dig the target can catch above her forehead in net zone 7.

Each player should go through the drill at least two to three times and keep a cumulative score.

Coaching Points: The coach controls the difficulty of the drill from free-ball passing to digging hard-driven attacks.

Variation: Change the angle of attacks by moving the coach to MF or RF attacking positions.

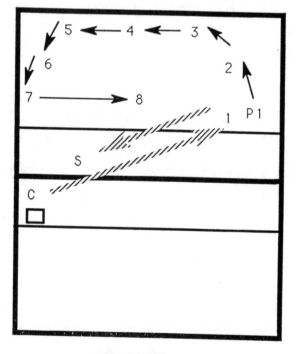

DRILL #50: JK'S DEFENSE MOVEMENT

Objective: To improve forward and backward defensive movement; to improve reading, covering, and court balancing.

Setup: 6–12 players; steady supply of volleyballs.

Description: Set up three players on defense, whose job it is to cover and balance the entire court . At the same time, position hitters on the opposite side of the court at LF.

The coach begins the drill by tossing a short or deep ball over the net. Next, the players must play the ball to the target, then immediately move into position to dig the attack from the coach's toss to the hitter. In order to score a point, the defenders must get both balls up to the target. If they do not touch a ball, the score reverts to zero. The defensive team must score 10 points in order to get out of the drill. The above maneuvers should be repeated from all hitting positions.

Coaching Points: It is a challenge for the defense to dig balls without the benefit of a block. The toss from the coach to the hitter will determine the difficulty of the drill (e.g., tosses off the net should be easier to defend).

Variation: Change the above attacks to backcourt attacks so that the defenders can practice digging balls that come from deeper in the court.

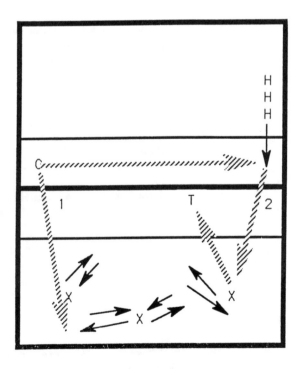

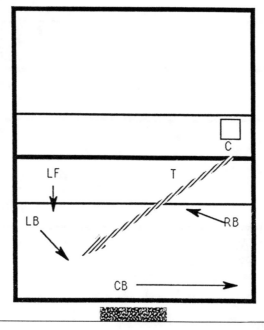

DRILL #51: BASE TO "D"

Objective: To help players develop efficient movement from base position to defensive position; to develop the proper weight shift toward the attack, at the moment of the attack.

Setup: Four players; steady supply of volleyballs.

Description: Set up the backcourt defensive team and the off-side blocker with a target on one side of the court. Players start at their base position and, on the coach's command, move to their defensive position.

Standing on a box across the net from the defenders, the coach attacks the ball from LF. The defenders then dig the ball to the target and return to their base position. This drill should be done from every possible attack option. Player movement will depend on the type of team defense played. (Note: The defense in the diagram below is a rotation-type defense.)

Coaching Points: The timing in this drill is very important. The coach must emphasize the importance of the players' weight shift toward the attack before the actual attack. Player movement should be stopped before the attack or on the coach's toss to herself or himself for a hit. Have the players touch the floor in front of them to help them learn the proper weight shift. The coach should use a quick attack to teach players to be set on attack, even if they do not get to their designated defensive position.

Variations: For more realistic game-like conditions, use a setter to set balls to the coach; or use hitters; or use both a setter and hitters.

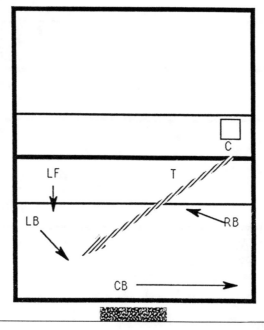

DRILL #52: PIT FOR TWO

Objective: To improve digging ability; to enhance the competitive drive for the relentless pursuit of all balls.

Setup: 6–12 players; steady supply of volleyballs.

Description: Set up two players on defense, whose job it is to cover and balance the entire court. The remaining players are to wait and shag balls. The coach begins the drill by delivering hard-driven spikes, as well as balls that are tough to retrieve, to the two diggers. Each digger must get the ball up in a settable position for her partner. As soon as the two diggers dig and overhead set a ball, they are out of the drill and must go to the end of the waiting line.

Coaching Points: The coach determines how long each team of two is in the pit by the difficulty of the attack. This drill is a relentless-pursuit drill with a built-in fatigue factor; therefore, it is essential that players never give up on a ball.

Variation: Change attacks so that they come from MF and RF. To make the drill more difficult, require teams to attack the ball back into their opponent's court before exiting the drill.

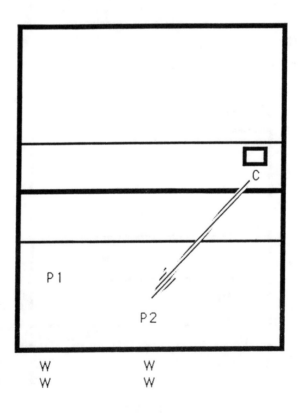

DRILL #53: DIGGING CIRCUIT

Objective: To improve forward and backward defensive movement, as well as digging, from all positions on the court.

Setup: 2–4 players; steady supply of volleyballs.

Description: Set up the players in a line at the RB corner. P1 starts the drill and will dig all positions from A through F before P2 begins the drill. C1 hits the ball down the line to position A, tips to B, hits to C, tips to D, and hits to E. C2 then hits to F and tosses a ball to G for P1 to attack over the net. C1 then attacks to A for P2, while P1 attacks the ball over the net. The drill continues in this manner.

Coaching Points: Emphasize proper mechanics both when moving forward and when retreating. In order to deter backpedaling, train the players in the fundamentals of the turn-and-go movement.

Variation: Change the attacks to RF and reverse the pattern of movement.

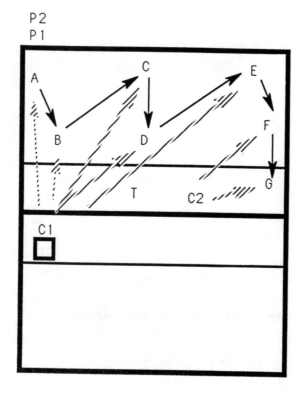

DRILL #54: PLUS TEN

Objective: To promote intensity and communication among players by focusing on the importance of pursuing every ball and not letting any ball touch the floor.

Setup: Four players; steady supply of volleyballs.

Description: Set up four players on defense, who are to cover and balance the entire court.

The coach runs this drill like a pit drill, hitting and tipping balls at players as fast as possible. Players must get every ball up to the target. The defensive team must earn 10 points in order to get out of the drill. Points are awarded as follows: 2 points for balls that go to the target; 1 point for balls that are playable; 0 points for balls that are touched but not playable; minus-1 point for balls dug over the net; and minus-2 points for balls that touch the floor before a player touches it.

As the drill progresses, the target constantly calls out the score so players and coaches know what the score is. The above maneuvers are repeated from all hitting positions.

Coaching Points: Since defense wins games, the goal of this drill bears remembering: To never allow a ball to touch the floor. The coach can make this drill easy to difficult.

Variations: Use a setter to determine if the balls are truly possible to set. In order to change the degree of difficulty of this drill, change the number of points required to exit the drill.

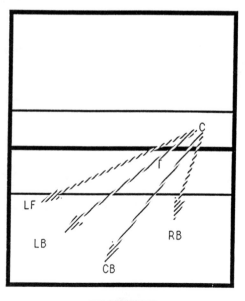

DRILL #55: HITTERS VS. DIGGERS

Objective: To promote game-like competition between hitters and diggers.

Setup: Eight players; steady supply of volleyballs.

Description: Players are divided into fairly equal groups of four. One group plays defense with three backcourt players and one blocker, while the other group hits at the defenders. The defense gets 1 point for every ball that is dug and playable and for every blocked ball. The defense also gets 1 point for hitter errors. The hitters get 1 point for every kill or ball that the coach determines is not playable. The defense must score 5 points to win, while the hitters must score 12.

Coaching Points: Digging balls with one blocker makes the defense cover open areas and involves reading the block as well as the hitter. Emphasize covering around the block.

Variation: Change the attacks so that they come from RF or MF.

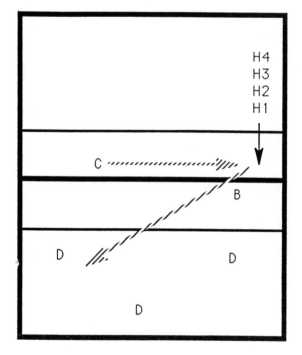

ATTACKING
DRILLS

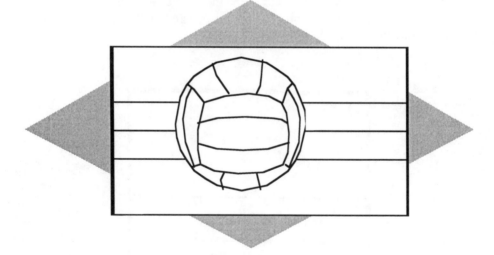

DRILL #56: CONSECUTIVE SWINGS

Objective: To help hitters learn the exacting mechanics of approaching and attacking the ball.

Setup: 2-4 players; steady supply of volleyballs.

Description: The coach will toss balls for hitters to approach and attack; the hitters will then transition off the net and approach and attack again. Each hitter will execute 25 attacks consecutively before exiting the drill. Two hitters are positioned in an attack line at LF, while another two hitters shag balls.

The coach starts the drill with tosses from zone 3 or 4. After the hitters have their timing down, the coach will work his or her way toward zone 7. For MF hitters and RF hitters, the coach will toss all the balls from zone 7. Each hitter should proceed through the drill twice.

Coaching Points: Emphasize the four-step approach for outside hitters, as well as the proper turn-and-go transition off the net.

Variations: Require hitters to hit a certain number of sets cross-court and a certain number down the line. Require hitters to execute a block jump after attacking. Also with this variation, require only 15 attacks from the hitters before they can exit the drill. In order to increase the difficulty of this drill, require that 25 balls be hit in the court before hitters can exit the drill.

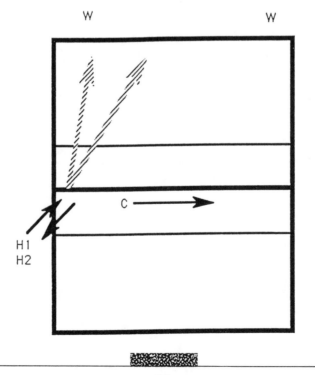

DRILL #57: PASS TO ATTACK

Objective: To help hitters learn the proper mechanics involved in passing and approaching and attacking the ball.

Setup: 5–7 players; steady supply of volleyballs.

Description: In this drill, the coach alternately delivers free balls or easy serves to two passers, who will then pass the ball to the setter and immediately move to attack at either LF or RF. The setter will deliver an outside set to the passer. The goal is to pass and attack 10 balls successfully before exiting the drill. Each pair of passers should go through the drill at least twice, alternating sides of the court.

Coaching Points: Emphasize passing the ball first, before moving to the attack position.

Variation: Add blockers to make the drill more game-like. In this scenario, pairs of players move from shaggers to blockers to passer/attacker after every completed drill.

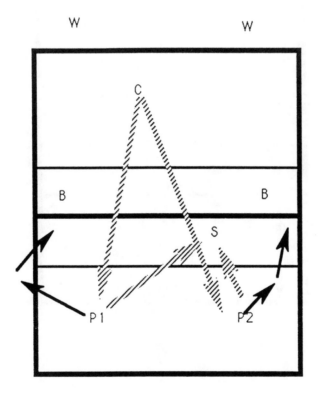

DRILL #58: DOUBLE HITS

Objective: To help hitters develop the stamina to endure long rallies.

Setup: Two players; steady supply of volleyballs.

Description: The coach begins the drill by tossing a set to H1, who hits and then sprints to the baseline as the coach is tossing to H2, who also hits and sprints to the baseline. The pair of hitters must hit 15 in a row in the court, both cross-court and down the line. This drill can be run for all front-row and back-row hitting positions.

Coaching Points: Emphasize proper mechanics, even as fatigue becomes a factor.

Variation: To increase the difficulty of the drill, add one or two blockers for the hitters to hit around.

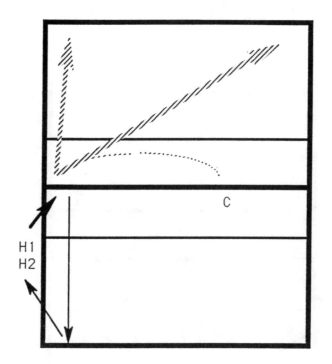

DRILL #59: THREE LINES HIGH HITTING

Objective: To help hitters learn the fundamentals of approaching and attacking the ball while reaching and hitting high.

Setup: Entire team; steady supply of volleyballs.

Description: Prior to the drill, the coach attaches elastic from antenna to antenna, 8–10 inches above the net. Hitters form three hitting lines at LF, MF, and RF, with a setter in net zone 7. The coach then begins the drill by tossing balls to the setter, who in turn sets each position alternately. The goal of the hitters is to attack the ball as high as possible, hitting above the elastic. The team gets a point for every ball it hits in the court that touches or goes above the elastic. The coach determines the number of points needed before the drill is ended.

Coaching Points: Emphasize hitting high to simulate hitting over a block. Raise or lower the elastic, depending on the success of the hitters.

Variation: To make the drill more competitive, deduct a point for every ball that is an attack error.

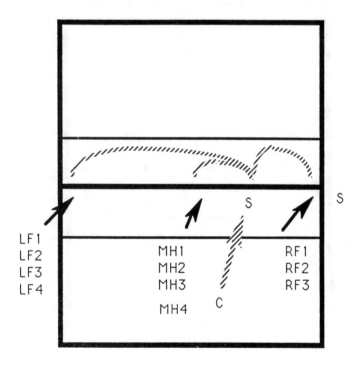

DRILL #60: ATTACK AND HIT THE OVERPASS

Objective: To train hitters to approach and attack the ball and immediately attack on an overpass.

Setup: 7–11 players; steady supply of volleyballs.

Description: C1 tosses balls for the setter to set three different hitters. C2 delivers second ball to the hitter from opposite side of the court, thus simulating an overpass (or dig) of the attacked ball. The hitter must successfully attack both balls before returning to the hitting line.

Coaching Points: Emphasize making the proper decision to attack or block the second ball or to back off the net and pass the second ball back to the setter.

Variations: Add blockers on the opposite side of the court to block both attacks. Run through all serve-receive combination plays so that the players learn to attack the overpass before they switch to front–row positions.

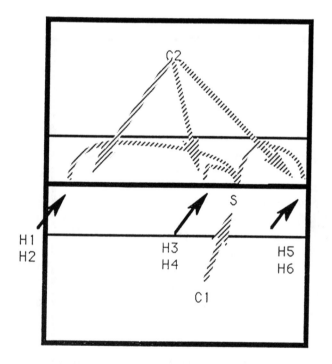

DRILL #61: TIP TO THE OPENING

Objective: To train hitters to tip to the opening in the opponent's defense when approaching and attacking the ball.

Setup: 6-9 players; steady supply of volleyballs.

Description: In this drill, the coach will toss balls for the setter to deliver to the hitters. First, though, the coach places a towel in the opponent's court to indicate the open spot for tipping. (Note: The coach's towel placement will change according to the opponent's defense.)

The attackers approach as if delivering a powerful spike, but instead, they tip the ball at the last moment. After tipping, the attackers become blockers. Ten successful tips to the open spot enable the hitter to exit the drill. This drill should be done at all three front-row positions.

Coaching Points: Utilize a blocker in this drill to force the hitter to reach high and thus ensure that her tip is not low. Instruct your players to use roll shots for sets that are too far off the net to tip legally.

Variations: Use the same drill to train players to make off-speed shots while using a normal spiking motion. Place the towel in the deep RB corner and run the drill to take the free ball over and deep.

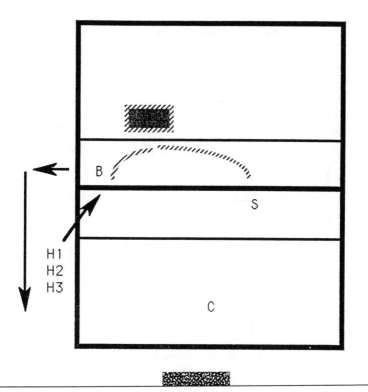

DRILL #62: MIDDLES ATTACK PASS

Objective: To help middle hitters develop a knack for watching the ball as it is passed to the setter and approaching to attack the quick set by using the correct timing.

Setup: 3–6 players; steady supply of volleyballs.

Description: The coach begins the drill by tossing a ball in a manner that simulates a pass or dig to the net. The MH then approaches and attacks the ball with a full arm swing and/or a tip.

At the beginning of the drill, the coach should toss perfect, antenna-high passes to net zone 7 until all the hitters have shown that they can successfully approach and attack the perfect pass. Once the hitters have proven their capability on the early tosses, the coach should then toss the passes higher and lower and to different zones of the net.

Coaching Points: This drill is excellent for training middle hitters to approach for the quick set. Since hitters often lose sight of the ball and look at the setter, this drill forces the hitters to follow the path of the ball. This drill will also train middle hitters who, too often, approach early or late.

Variation: The coach tosses to passers or hits at diggers, who pass the ball for the middles to attack.

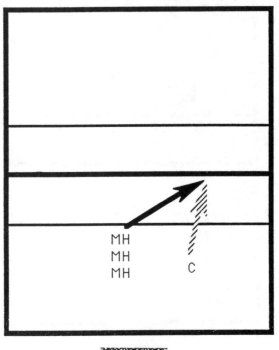

DRILL #63: TRIPLE HIT

Objective: To help hitters develop their attacking skills by having them successfully attack three balls in succession, and in a game-like situation.

Setup: 4–8 players; steady supply of volleyballs.

Description: H2 tosses the ball to the setter, who sets H1, who attacks the ball cross-court. The coach then tosses a simulated overpass to H1, who attacks from the other side of the net. H2 then tosses another ball to the setter, who again sets H1. H1 must then transition off the net and touch H2 before approaching to attack. After three successful attacks, H1 returns to the end of the hitting line. H2 then replaces H1 and runs through the same triple-hit drill.

Coaching Points: This drill can be conducted so that players do not rotate to the end of the line unless they successfully attack all three balls or unless the ball is put in play again where their error occurred.

Variation: Add a blocker to the drill and run the drill at all three hitting positions.

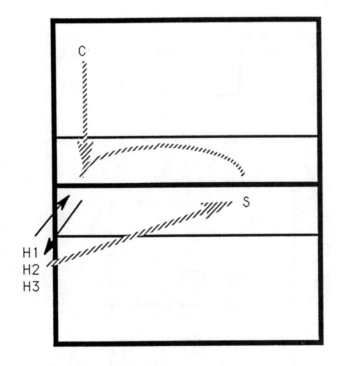

DRILL #64: OUTSIDES' FIVE-POINT

Objective: To help your outside hitters develop their transition attacking skills while hitting both cross-court and down the line.

Setup: Six players; steady supply of volleyballs.

Description: The coach (C1) sets up both sides of the court with a LF, a LB, and a S (or RF). The coach also dictates whether the drill will be run with the goal of hitting cross-court or down the line. (The diagram below depicts cross-court attacking.) C1 puts the ball in play to either side with a down-ball attack over the net to either the LB or LF, who passes the ball to the setter, who sets the LF, who attacks cross-court.

As long as the players can continue digging and attacking, the ball will remain in play. A point is scored only when the ball hits the floor in the cross-court portion of the opponent's court. No point is awarded for any ball that falls down the line. C2, who is standing behind the baseline at mid-court, will score the game out loud. C1 should alternate putting the ball in play to both teams. C1 may or may not choose to allow tips.

Coaching Points: This is an excellent drill for training outside hitters to hit different angles against one blocker and cross-court defenders. It is also a good drill for training RF non-setters to deliver high-outside sets in transition. The drill rewards good defense by allowing attackers another opportunity to put the ball away for a point after a good dig.

Variations: Add an additional digger for the CB position. Mirror the drill so it is run for RF attackers.

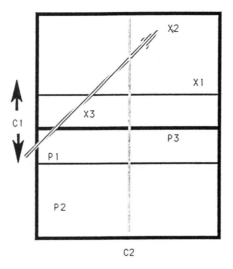

DRILL #65: MIDDLES' FIVE-POINT

Objective: To help your middle hitters develop their transition attacking skills by communicating with the setter on every play.

Setup: Eight players; steady supply of volleyballs.

Description: The coach sets up both sides of the court with two diggers, an MH, and an S. The coach then begins the drill by putting balls in play to either side with a down-ball attack over the net to either back-row player. Players pass the ball to the setter, who sets the MH, who communicates which set to deliver.

The ball remains in play as long as the players can continue digging and attacking. A point is scored only when the ball hits the floor as a result of an MH's attack or block. When either MH scores five points, the drill ends.

In this drill, the coach should alternate putting the ball in play to both teams. The coach may also choose to disallow tips. Also, if the dig does not allow the setter to set, the middle hitter, the setter should set the back-row diggers for a back-row attack.

Coaching Points: This is an excellent drill for training middle hitters to hit different sets in transition and to communicate with the setter. It also rewards good defense, since attackers earn bonus tries for points if their team digs the opponent successfully.

Variations: Add an additional digger to play CB. Restrict the MH to scoring only with a specific set (e.g., only 1's in the middle can score).

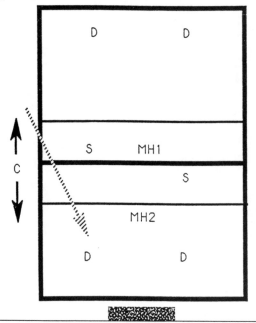

BLOCKING
DRILLS

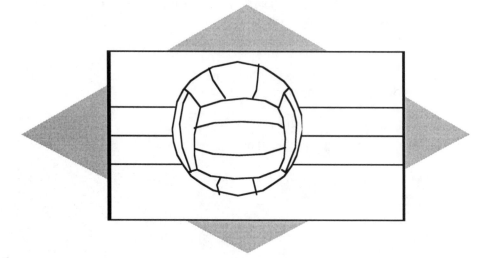

DRILL #66: BLOCKING WORKOUT

Objective: To help your players learn how to shape their body when they are blocking; to teach them what their bodies should feel like whenever they execute a block.

Setup: Entire team; no volleyballs.

Description: This is a building-block–type of workout (i.e., what your players use in Step 1, they must also use in Step 2; what they use in Steps 1 and 2, they must use in Step 3, etc.). This entire workout takes about 20 minutes and will be intense (causing tension from head to toe). When you instruct your athletes to perform the following steps, remind them that they can do the first four steps either sitting or standing:

- Full-finger abduction: Spread your fingers out as far as they will go, tense them for three seconds, and shake them out. Repeat 3–5 times.

- Slight wrist extension: At the same time you abduct your fingers, extend your wrists into the opponent's court (no slapping allowed), tense them for three seconds, and shake them out. Repeat 3–5 times.

- Shoulder protraction and elevation: Push your shoulders forward and up into your ears without lowering your head, do Steps 1 and 2, tense and hold. Repeat 3–5 times.

- Touch the tips of your thumbs together, spreading your fingers apart as wide as possible. Repeat with eyes closed.

- Do 10 crunch-type sit-ups, holding each one for 10 seconds. Do steps 1–4 and bend at the waist until your upper body comes off the floor.

- Still in a sit-up position, with your back flat on the floor, do Steps 1–4 and squeeze your cheeks together.

- Stay in the sit-up position, straighten your legs, point your toes, and raise your arms overhead, as in steps 1–4.

- Stay in the sit-up position described in Step 7, and then lower your chin to your chest, but keep your eyes up.

- Roll over into a hollowed-out, push-up–type position with your buttocks high off the floor. Hold for three seconds and repeat 3–5 times.

- Still in the push-up position, slide your arms down and do a regular push-up, but with your buttocks still high in the air, and then have a partner slowly slide your legs back until you are flat on the floor. Repeat three times.

- Do a fingertip push-up and repeat Step 10.

- Roll back over into a sitting position and pike (straighten both your arms and legs), while a partner attempts to pull your legs and arms apart.

- Stand up and assume a blocking stance while on your toes. Hold for three seconds and repeat 3–5 times.

- In front of a mirror, jump into a blocking stance and hold for three seconds after landing. Repeat 3–5 times.

- From various contorted positions, and on the coach's "block" command, assume the proper blocking stance on your toes. Hold for three seconds and repeat 3–5 times.

Coaching Points: This workout should be done daily by players at the beginning or lower levels and two to three times a week for more advanced players. This workout trains the body to be a "blocking machine" and not just a flimsy target. Incorporate what this drill teaches into the remainder of your blocking drills. Players need to know how their body should feel.

Variation: Do one to five different steps daily, keeping in mind the building-block philosophy.

DRILL #67: BLOCKING: FOOTWORK, CONDITIONING, AND COMMUNICATION

Objective: To help your middle blockers develop the proper footwork for closing and communicating with your outside blockers.

Setup: 3–4 players per half-court; no volleyballs.

Description: Set up three blockers at the net. All three blockers (this drill can be done with all middle blockers or with middles and outsides) take a blocking position at the net.

The MB starts the drill with a block jump at the CF position, then moves laterally to block with the RF blocker, back to the middle, then to the left to block with the LF blocker. As the MB returns to the middle of the net, she has completed one trip, or four block jumps. However, she must complete 10 trips before exiting the drill. The MB then switches positions with an outside blocker, who then becomes the MB. Repeat this drill so that all blockers do the drill a total of three times.

Coaching Points: This is a conditioning drill for middle blockers, but proper footwork and blocking form should be emphasized. Be sure that the outside blockers communicate as they would in a real game (e.g., calling out, "ready," "go," or "wait, wait, go") so that the block is a solid one.

Variations: Use the outside blockers at LF and RF to work on communication and setting a good block. Place a setter on the opposite side of the court, who will set all three options while allowing the MB to read and move.

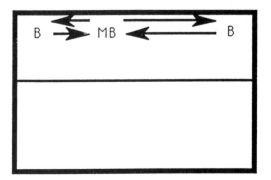

DRILL #68: SHADOW BLOCKING

Objective: To teach your players where their block should be set in relation to their opponent's approach.

Setup: 2-6 players; no volleyballs.

Description: Set up an equal number of players opposite each other at the net. On one side will be attackers; on the other side will be blockers. The attackers will take their normal approach, while, at the same time, the blockers will try to intercept the attackers in a direct line with the attackers' approach. The attackers will proceed under the net, continuing their line of approach. If the attackers do not "run into" the blockers, then the blockers have not correctly intercepted the attackers.

The coach should instruct the attackers to vary their approaches from straight in to approaches that come in from different angles. After a while, the players should switch roles.

Coaching Points: Keep in mind that beginning blockers will often set a block where they happen to be standing, and thus will not move to intercept the attacker's path. Since no volleyballs are used in this drill, it helps the blockers focus on the hitter.

Variation: For a more realistic, game-like practice, put a ball into the equation by allowing the setter to set the hitter.

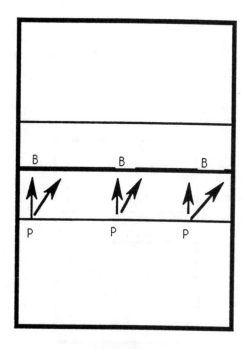

DRILL #69: PREPARATION VS. SETTER

Objective: To train your blockers to be in the ready position as the ball is passed to the setter; to help them learn to prepare to move as the setter contacts the ball; to teach them to anticipate where the set may go by reading the setter.

Setup: From four players to the entire team; three volleyballs.

Description: The coach and setter should set up on one side of the net, with the other players on the opposite side of the net. If only three blockers are utilized in this drill, they should be placed at the net, in their normal front-row positions. If more than three blockers are used, they should be positioned behind the front-row players, in their normal front-row positions. The blockers will assume the blocking-ready position as the coach tosses the ball to the setter to begin the drill. On contact with the setter's hands, the blockers will bend their knees slightly and be ready to move.

In this, the first phase of the drill, the setter will simply catch the ball above her forehead and return it to the coach. This phase should be repeated until all the blockers are executing properly. Also, the lines should be rotated every five passes so that all the blockers eventually rotate to the net.

Phase 2 requires that the setter set to RF and LF, while the blockers take one big step in the direction of the set and then execute a block jump before returning to the starting position. In order to get the proper results, this drill should be repeated as many times as necessary.

Coaching Points: The missing ingredient in successful blocking often proves to be a lack of blocker preparation. Keep in mind, therefore, that this aspect of blocking must be ingrained in your blockers until it becomes a habit.

Variation: In order to make this drill more game-like, utilize a passer instead of the coach's toss.

DRILL #70: ONE-ON-ONE AT THE NET

Objective: To help your blockers develop the skill of reading the action of the hitter; to enhance their ability to block balls one-on-one.

Setup: 3–4 players; steady supply of volleyballs.

Description: In this drill, the coach stands on a box at the net and repeatedly tosses the ball up and attacks it over the net at the blocker. The blocker, meantime, must successfully block 10 balls before exiting the drill to become a shagger or a feeder. The coach turns his or her body in the direction of the intended spike, so that the blockers must learn to read the hitter and intercept the ball in the proper direction. Three of these drills can be run on the same court simultaneously.

Coaching Points: Emphasize to your blockers the importance of their penetrating over the net so that they can take away the low, hard-driven attack. Discourage your blockers from thinking that their goal should be to jump and reach as high as possible.

Variation: Lower the net and have your players work one-on-one against each other at the net. In this variation, the players should toss the ball to themselves and then hit the ball into the block.

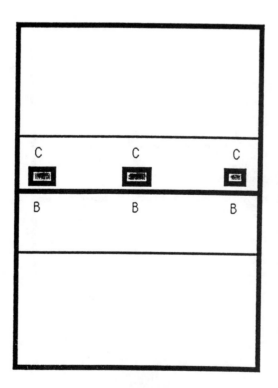

DRILL #71: BLIND BLOCKING

Objective: To train your blockers to watch the opposing hitter when blocking, instead of focusing on just the ball.

Setup: 2–4 players per court; steady supply of volleyballs.

Description: The coach sets up a hitter and a blocker opposite each other at the net and positions himself or herself behind the blocker, armed with a supply of balls.

In this drill, the hitter may use a normal approach or may simply stand three feet from the net and jump and attack. The coach begins the drill by tossing balls from behind the blocker, balls that the hitter is to attack. The blocker will watch the attacker and attempt to block without benefit of seeing the ball in flight to the hitter. This drill can be run on both sides of the court.

Coaching Points: Many beginning and higher-level players have tunnel vision when they block and, therefore, they watch only the flight of the ball as it approaches the hitter. This tunnel vision makes it difficult for them to time their block and also makes it almost impossible for them to set a proper block. This drill successfully takes the ball out of the equation and forces the blocker to watch the hitter.

Variation: Run this drill at all front-row blocking and attacking positions.

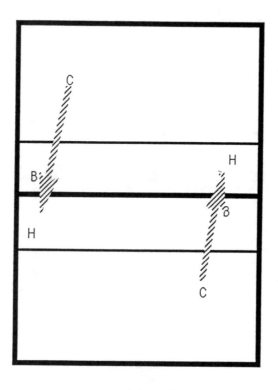

DRILL #72: PENETRATE THE NET

Objective: To train your blockers to reach over the net to intercept the ball before it passes over the net.

Setup: 6–9 players; no volleyballs.

Description: The coach runs a piece of elastic from one antenna to the other, about eight inches above the net. The antennae are then left unattached to the bottom of the net and held by two coaches. The coaches tilt the antennae so that the elastic is over the opponent's court (i.e., the tops of the antennae are tilted over the opponent's court).

The players, meanwhile, are positioned in three lines, at their normal front-row blocking positions. As the drill gets under way, each player must mock-block five times—making sure to touch the elastic each time—and then proceed to the end of the line. This maneuver should be repeated 5–10 times.

Coaching Points: This is an excellent drill, because it lets your players evaluate whether they are penetrating the net when blocking. Emphasize the art of "placing" the hands over the net, a skill that reduces the number of net fouls.

Variation: The net may be lowered, and/or the height of the elastic changed, depending on the players' skill level.

DRILL #73: BAM THROUGH THE BLOCK

Objective: To train your blockers to put up a solid outside block.

Setup: 6–10 players; a steady supply of volleyballs.

Description: On one side of the court, the coach sets up a LF and a setter; on the other side, a RF and MB and two backcourt players. The coach begins the drill by tossing the ball to the setter, who sets the LF attacker. The opposite MB closes to the RF and attempts to block the hitter.

The hitter's job is to hit every ball line or seam (or "bam through the block"). The hitter scores a point for every attack that hits the floor line or seam, or for any blocking error. The defending team scores on every blocked ball and every dug ball. Balls hit cross-court do not result in a score for either team. The winner is the first team to score 10 points, at which time the attacker switches with a defender.

Coaching Points: Blockers rarely get the opportunity to practice blocking, because hitters are trained to hit around the block. This drill overcomes that handicap by allowing the blockers to evaluate their effectiveness. Point out to your players that on perfect passes, the MB may not leave (to close to the outside) until the setter releases the ball.

Variations: The coach can vary his or her passes to the setter, thus allowing the MB to read and anticipate the outside set. In order to make the drill more game-like, add a RF attacker and a LF blocker.

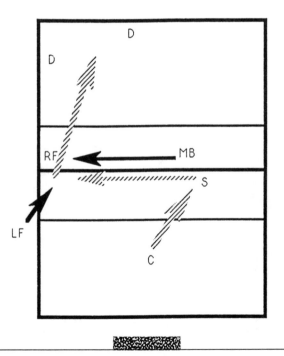

DRILL #74: LF BLOCKING

Objective: To train LF blockers to block their own hitter and also help the MB block the middle hitter.

Setup: 4–6 players; a steady supply of volleyballs.

Description: The LF players line up at the LF blocking position. On the opposite side of the court, two coaches are stationed on boxes at the RF and MF positions.

As the drill begins, the first LF blocker attempts to block C1's attack and then quickly moves in to block a second attack by C2. The first LF waits in the middle for the next LF to close to her to block the second attack. The first LF then returns to the blocking line. Each player should rotate through the drill 10 or more times, scoring points for every successful block in which she participates.

Coaching Points: Instruct the LF blocker to watch the hitter and take away her anticipated angle. Be sure that the LF takes one huge lateral step to close to the MB to block the second attack.

Variation: Make the drill more game-like by removing the coaches and adding two hitters and a setter and repeating this drill as a live-action drill.

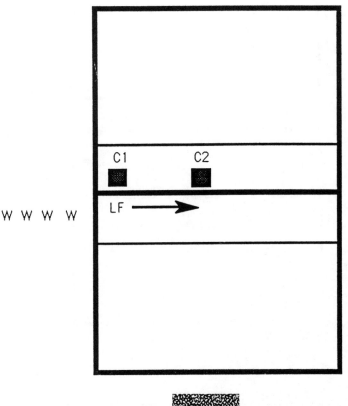

DRILL #75: ONE VS. THREE

Objective: To enhance the conditioning of the MB; to improve her movement skills.

Setup: 5–12 players; a steady supply of volleyballs.

Description: The coach sets up three hitting lines, along with a setter, on one side of the net; on the other side, the coach places a MB at the MF position.

The coach begins the drill by tossing the ball to the setter, who then sets any front-row position. The MB goes to the position of the set and attempts to block the ball. Upon landing, the MB returns quickly to MF, and then the coach tosses another ball. This drill continues until either a specified number of attacks is achieved, or until the MB has blocked five balls.

Coaching Points: Encourage the MB to take a big first step to the outside and to also penetrate the net on every attempt.

Variation: Add RF and LF blockers, so that the MB closes to them, and require the blockers to block 10 balls before switching to attackers.

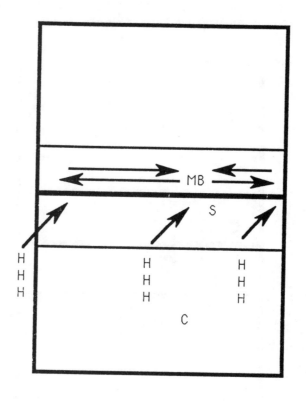

COMBINATION
AND
TRANSITION
DRILLS

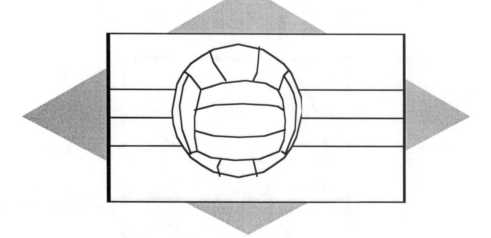

DRILL #76: OVER-THE-NET PEPPER

Objective: To enhance ball-handling skills in a game-like situation utilizing a net.

Setup: 4–6 players per half-court; 1 volleyball per half-court.

Description: Divide the court in half lengthwise by placing an additional antenna at mid-court. This drill can be run with two or three players per team; each team plays in a designated half-court. The ball may be put in play by the coach, or it may be served.

During this drill, the players play regular volleyball in terms of pass, set, and hit, but they must also switch positions after sending the ball over the net. For example: The ball is thrown to P1, who passes the ball to P2. P2 sets the ball back to P1, who hits the ball over the net to X1. P1 and P2 then exchange positions. X1 passes to X2, who sets X1, who hits the ball over the net to P2. X1 and X2 then exchange positions.

The players must remember that every set should be five feet off the net. (The diagram below depicts both two-on-two and three-on-three over-the-net pepper.)

Coaching Points: If your goal is to work on serve and receive, allow your players to serve; otherwise, toss the ball into play. In additon, instruct your players to attempt to keep the ball in play rather than terminate the action.

Variations: Any number of players may be involved in this drill (e.g., three players may play against two). Also, as soon as one team loses a point, another team of players may rotate onto the court.

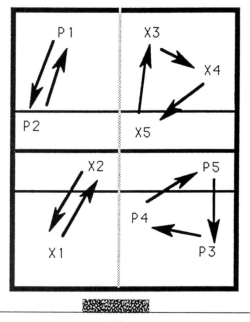

DRILL #77: LISA'S PHBDHB

Objective: To train the outside hitter in a game-like sequence of skills.

Setup: 2–4 players; a steady supply of volleyballs.

Description: Two players, an outside hitter and a setter, participate in this drill. In order to complete the drill, the hitter must successfully execute consecutive touches on the ball—a Pass, a Hit, a Block, a Dig, a Hit, and a Block.

This drill is initiated by a serve. Following that initial serve, however, all executions are initiated by coaches standing on boxes. If the hitter misses any part of the sequence, she must start over. As depicted in the diagram below, P1 passes the served ball to the setter. The setter then sets P1 a high-outside set that P1 attacks over the net. P1 blocks a ball attacked by C1. P1 then transitions to defense to dig a ball from C2 to the setter, who delivers another high-outside set that P1 attacks over the net. P1 then blocks another ball from C1 and completes the drill. P1 then becomes the server, and the server becomes the hitter.

Coaching Points: This drill requires game-like movement patterns. Therefore, the coach should emphasize the proper footwork necessary for transitioning off the net.

Variations: Replace C2 with live attackers who hit to a designated zone. Require the hitter to vary her attacking zones.

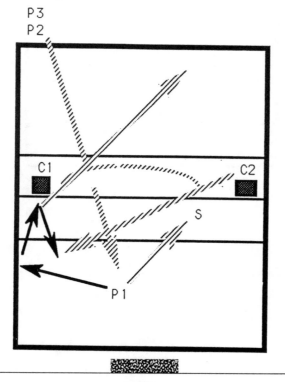

DRILL #78: CONCENTRATION

Objective: To enhance player communication and focus.

Setup: 3–9 players; a steady supply of volleyballs.

Description: From a prone position at the baseline, three players prepare for the start of the drill. The coach then slaps the ball and sends a high free ball into the players' court. Players must pass, set, and hit in order, and each player must also execute each skill by the time three balls have been put in play by the coach. If a player has to repeat a skill, the drill begins again.

During the drill, the players must communicate in order to determine whose turn it is to pass or set or hit. The players must then return to the prone position after each attack over the net. After the three players successfully complete three contacts in order, three more players take the court and replace them.

Coaching Points: Allow your players to problem-solve in this drill. Give very little instruction. The players will be required to communicate on every ball touch, a habit which should carry over to live game action.

Variation: Require that the attack be a backcourt attack.

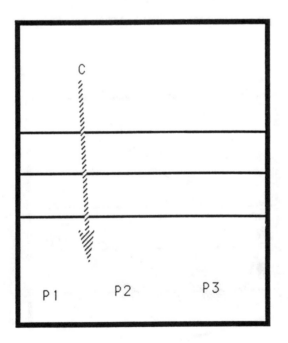

DRILL #79: RECEIVE AND BACKCOURT ATTACK

Objective: To practice passing the serve and getting into position for backcourt attacking.

Setup: Six players; a steady supply of volleyballs.

Description: Divide the court lengthwise by placing another antenna on the net at mid-court. In this drill, the servers serve the ball to the passers, who pass to the setter, who sets back to the backcourt passer, who attacks. (The players should switch positions after 10 successful attacks.) As the diagram below shows, P1 serves to P2, who passes to P3, who sets P2, who attacks from behind the attack line. The X players do the same. Team X beats Team P if X finishes the drill before P (i.e., all three players complete 10 successful attacks).

Coaching Point: This drill is conducive to working on receiving serves with the overhead pass.

Variation: Remove the mid-court antenna and have servers serve cross-court.

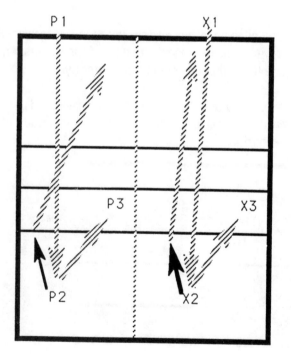

DRILL #80: THREE OUT OF FIVE

Objective: To improve the teams' on side-out ability; to enhance their ability to execute tough serves.

Setup: 12 players; 4 volleyballs.

Description: Set up one side of the court in the starting serve-receive positions; set up the other side with three back-row and three front-row players.

In this drill, the receivers attempt to pass and to run serve-receive plays for three side-outs before the other team can serve an ace. The servers get five chances to serve an ace. If they fail, they must run sprints, do sit-ups, do push-ups, etc. If the players on the receiving team fail to get three side-outs, then they must also run sprints, etc. If neither side is successful, everyone must run sprints. If the receiving team is successful, its players rotate to the next serve-receive formation.

The serving team, meanwhile, switches back-row and front-row positions so that everyone can serve. The drill is completed once the receiving team has run three side-out plays in all six rotations.

Coaching Points: This drill allows the coach to evaluate the strength or weakness of each serve-receive rotation, as well as the strength of the servers. Analyze each side-out play and change those that do not work consistently.

Variations: Require the receiving team to side-out from a designated position (e.g., only attacks from the middle score); or, at least one of the three side-outs must come from a designated position.

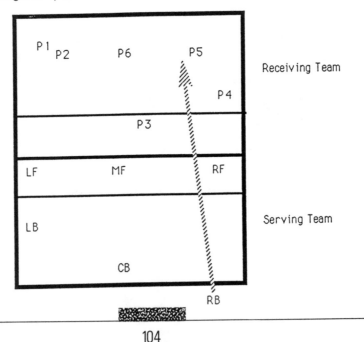

DRILL #81: QUEEN OF THE COURT

Objective: To improve your players' ability to maintain solid ball control; to enhance their conditioning.

Setup: 10–12 players; 3–4 balls.

Description: Teams of two or three players set up on opposite sides of the court and play two-on-two or three-on-three, with the games initiated by a serve. The team that wins the point either stays on the "Queen" side of the court or sprints under the net to the Queen side. The losers, however, sprint to the end of the line. The next (waiting) team serves to the Queens, and the drill continues until a team is able to stay on the Queen side for the designated number of points (either consecutive or total points).

Coaching Points: Two-player teams will mean more sprinting and less ball-in-play time. Three-player teams will be more successful keeping the ball in play.

Variations: Allow the waiting team to serve the ball immediately after the ball in play touches the ground. This variation will speed up the drill immensely. Also, allow only backcourt attacking as a means to working on this ball-control aspect of the game.

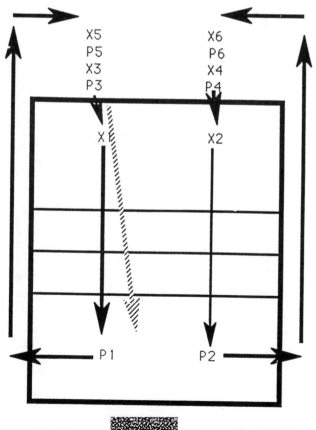

DRILL #82: FIVE-ON-FIVE DIG OR DIE

Objective: To improve digging in single-block situations; to promote an attitude of relentless pursuit.

Setup: 10 players; 10 volleyballs.

Description: Position five players on each side of the court without middle blockers. Allow the offense to pass with two to four players. X4 always hits LF, and X1 can hit RF or RB, although technically, they are a backcourt player. The coach alternates putting the ball in play to each side. Rally scoring is in place, but if a ball hits the floor before being touched by a player, that team forfeits all the points it has already accumulated. Example: The score is 14-1, and, without being touched, the ball hits the floor of the team that is winning. That makes the score 0-2.

Coaching Points: Encourage a never-say-die attitude among your defenders. This drill emphasizes the importance of going after every ball.

Variations: Remove the RF attacker, which will force the setter to be offensive. In order to produce longer rallies, limit hitters to off-speed attacks.

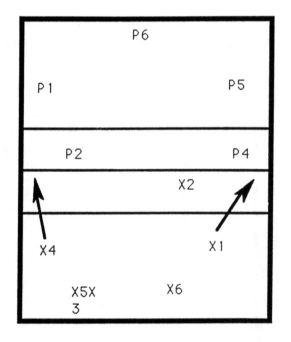

DRILL #83: TWO VS. SIX

Objective: To improve the hitter's ability to score versus team defense; to effect a smooth team transition to offense.

Setup: Eight players; a steady supply of volleyballs.

Description: On one side of the court, set up six players in team defensive positions. On the other side of the court, set up a setter, a hitter, and a coach. The coach begins the drill by tossing the ball to the setter, who will set the hitter. The hitter can then hit from anywhere and, in the process, will communicate with the setter.

In order to score a point, the hitter must kill three balls consecutively. The hitter's goal is to score six points before the defensive team earns 25 denials. A denial is earned each time the defensive team puts the ball away on the hitter's court. The defensive team also rotates after every big point scored by the hitter.

Coaching Points: The coach determines the pace of this drill, which can be made more competitive by using a flip scoreboard. Also, as soon as the ball is down or is returned over the net by the defensive team, the coach should initiate the next toss to the setter.

Variations: Add another hitter to the drill and follow the same format. Also, if it is necessary to shorten the drill, simply change the scoring system.

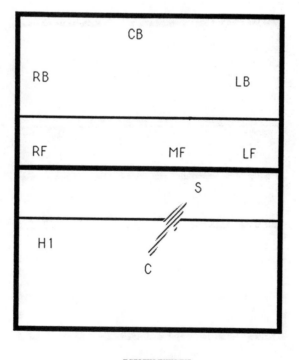

DRILL #84: RIGHT-SIDE TRANSITION

Objective: To train the RF and RB players to coordinate each other's movements in order to make quick transitions off the opponent's LF tips and RF cross-court attacks.

Setup: 2–4 players; a steady supply of volleyballs.

Description: On one side of the court are two coaches, who take positions on boxes at LF and RF. On the other side are a RF and a RB. The RF starts the drill by attempting to block a tip by C1. The RB passes the tipped ball to the RF, who sets or attacks the pass. Immediately, both players shift to their defensive positions, anticipating an attack from their opponent's RF (or, in this case, C2). C2 then attacks the ball cross-court to either right-side player, who in turn digs while the other right-side player sets the dig.

The above sequence should be repeated until a certain number of balls (decided on by the coaches) have been dug and set successfully.

Coaching Points: When training more than two right-side players, the waiting players can act as targets for the set; they can then rotate in after every two attacks from the coaches.

Variation: Replace the coaches with two hitters and a setter on the opponent's side. Instruct the LF hitter to tip only, and the RF hitter to attack cross-court.

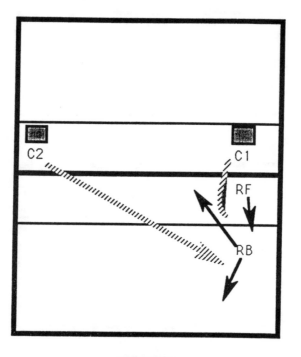

DRILL #85: SEVEN PLAYER

Objective: To improve the ability to make and dig successful back-row attacks; to enhance the conditioning of your setter and hitters.

Setup: 7–10 players; a steady supply of volleyballs.

Description: On one side of the court, set up two backcourt diggers, two hitters, and a setter. On the other side, set up two diggers. The ball is put in play by the coach, with a down or free ball to the setter's side of the court. Diggers pass the ball to the setter, who sets either hitter a backcourt set. After attacking the ball over the net, all three front-row players proceed under the net to the other side of the court. The setter receives the dig from the backcourt and sets another 10-foot-line set to either hitter, who then attacks over the net. The players proceed under the net as before.

Diggers, meanwhile, remain stationary and do not change courts. If the setter is unable to set the hitters, she may set the back-row diggers, who then attack the ball over the net. Most important, the goal is to keep the ball in play. When the ball is mishandled, the coach puts the ball in play where the error occurred, and play continues. The three players can be the runners for a set amount of time, or for a certain number of successful attacks. Diggers become attackers, attackers become opposite-court diggers, and a setter subs in. Two waiting players take the diggers' open spots, and the drill starts once more.

Coaching Points: Allow non-setters to work as setters in this drill so that they can work on handling the ball in a stressful situation. This drill is an excellent ball-control drill.

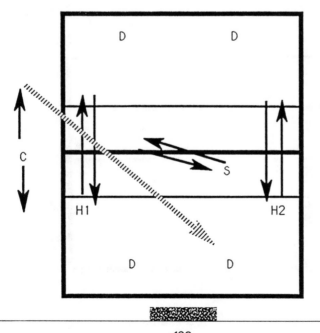

DRILL #86: BACKCOURT TRIPLES

Objective: To train in a game-like situation that stresses ball control while passing and digging. (With only three players covering the court, the players are forced to be mobile and to cover a large area.)

Setup: 8–12 players; a steady supply of volleyballs.

Description: On both sides of the court, set up a hitter, three backcourt players, and a line of subs. The coach tosses or hits at either backcourt; either backcourt then passes to the setter, who delivers a set to the attack line. The ball is played out until an error is made. The player committing the error is replaced by a sub on her side and must go to the end of the sub line. The coach feeds the next ball to the team that is winning, while the sub takes her place on the opposite side.

Player errors include the following: missing a pass or a dig, passing or digging over the net, hitting the ball into the net or out of bounds, and taking a free ball over that could have been attacked.

Coaching Points: Setters may be replaced if more setters are available, or all the team members may act as setters. This is a good drill for beginners, who will be able to practice their ball control and backcourt attacking.

Variation: Take the setters out of this drill and play true "triples."

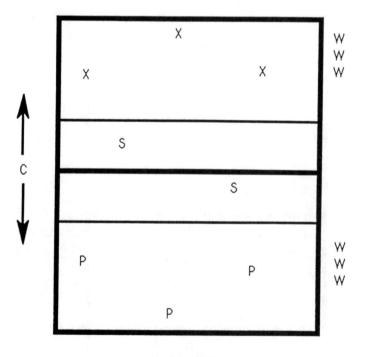

DRILL #87: VIRUS

Objective: To help develop the ability to transfer every bad pass into some type of attack.

Setup: 6–12 players; 6 volleyballs.

Description: The coach sets up one side of the court with the starting team in serve-receive position. C1 is positioned in the middle of the serve-receive formation and will act as the virus. C2 begins the drill by tossing or serving to C1, who intentionally makes a bad pass. C1's pass is considered the first contact, and the team has two more contacts in which to send the ball over the net.

Coaching Points: Players at higher levels of skill should be able to turn every ball into an attack. At beginning levels of play, however, the coach should direct the players to take the ball over the net with the most difficult free ball possible (e.g., take the ball either deep or to the RB corner). The coach controls the difficulty by varying the types of bad passes.

Variations: Place the teams in defensive positions rather than serve-receive positions, with the coach in the middle as the virus. Also, place another team of six , along with a virus, and play the ball out.

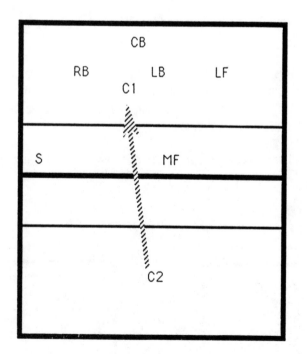

DRILL #88: TIP TO COVER

Objective: To improve your team's ability to cover the attacker at each hitting position.

Setup: Six players per half-court; one volleyball.

Description: The coach sets up the team in serve-receive formation and then begins the drill by tossing the ball to a passer, who in turn, passes to the setter, who then sets the LF hitter. At this point, all the players move to cover the hitter in their designated positions. The LF hitter, instead of attacking the ball over the net, tips the ball back to her covering teammates. The cover players call the ball, pass it to the setter's zone, and the setter again sets the LF. The goal of this drill is to keep the ball in play and not allow it to hit the floor. Teams of six compete against each other to see which group can keep the ball in play the longest.

In the next phase of the drill, the coach has the players shift to their defensive positions and go through the same sequence as before, except this time they will be starting from their defensive positions instead of a serve-receive formation. After all the players have become comfortable with their covering positions for LF, the coach instructs the setter to set the MF hitter, and the sequence starts over again. After she covers from both the serve-receive and defensive positions, the setter is then instructed by the coach to set the RF hitter.

All of the above steps should be repeated for all six rotations, as well as all play combinations.

Coaching Points: This is a good drill for teaching coverage positions early in the season. Late in the season, and at higher levels of play, the coach may instruct the setter to set any hitter in any sequence. Emphasize to your players that they should stay low to cover and be set at the time of the hitter's jump.

Variation: Set the backcourt hitters and instruct them to tip the ball forward and right or left, but not over the net.

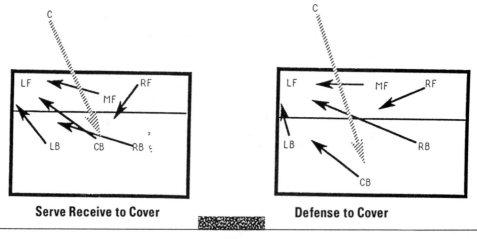

Serve Receive to Cover   **Defense to Cover**

DRILL #89: DIAMOND

Objective: To improve the ability to move quickly and efficiently to the defensive position and back to the base position every time the setter touches the ball.

Setup: 10 players; 1 volleyball.

Description: On one side of the court, the coach places an "X" on the floor at each of the six base, or starting, positions for the defensive team, and also places six defensive players in their position and on their "X." On the other side of the court, the coach sets up a passer, a setter, and two hitters (LF and RF). The coach instructs the defenders to stay on their "X" every time the setter contacts the ball, and then move to their defensive position on the basis of where the setter sets the ball.

The players on the opposite side of the court initiate the drill with an overhead pass from the passer (P) to the setter (S), who sets either hitter. The hitter jump-sets the ball back to the passer, and the defending blockers jump to block. The passer then passes the ball back to the setter, and the drill continues. After a designated period of time (maybe two to five minutes), the front-row and back-row players should switch positions.

Coaching Points: This is a great drill for teaching defensive responsibilites and movement back to base position. It is also a great conditioning drill, as long as you encourage your players to work hard and be set in their defensive position when the hitter jumps and back in their base position on every setter contact.

Variation: In order to work on your team's defensive position versus a middle attack, add an MH on the opposite side.

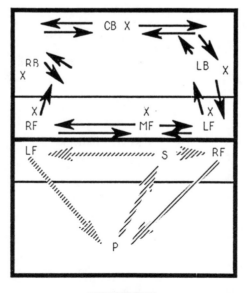

SIX-ON-SIX DRILLS

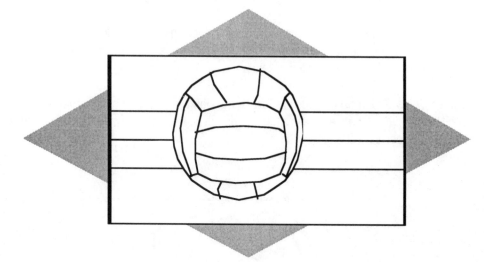

DRILL #90: FREE-BALL PASSING PROGRESSION

Objective: To train your players to perfect their free-ball passing by progressing from easy to more difficult skills.

Setup: 10–12 players; a steady supply of volleyballs.

Description: This drill is conducted in four phases:

- Phase 1: At the outset, two lines of passers and a target are in place. The coach begins the drill by tossing or hitting an easy free ball to one of the passers, who passes to the target and then becomes the target herself. After a predetermined number of perfect passes or a set amount of time, the next phase begins.

- Phase 2: The coach replaces the target with a setter, and the setter sets to the passer, who has become a catcher at RF or LF.

- Phase 3: Add RF and LF hitters, who attack the setter's sets over the net. The passer proceeds to the hitter's line after passing.

- Phase 4: The MH attacks quicks off of free-ball passes.

Coaching Points: Free-ball passes should be perfect passes. This drill eventually progresses to the the point where it helps evaluate passes by requiring that they be "good enough" to set the MH a quick set.

Variation: Instead of having players rotate through the drill, and before they switch positions, have the passers pass a certain number of balls, and have the hitters hit a certain number as well.

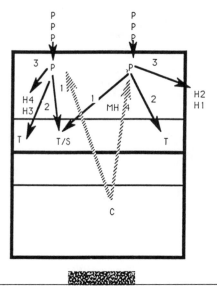

DRILL #91: SIDE-OUT TO ROTATE (AROUND THE WORLD)

Objective: To help develop the ability to handle pressure on serve-receive patterns and come up with a crucial side-out; to foster a competitive spirit; to improve passing skills.

Setup: 12 players; 1 volleyball.

Description: This drill is modeled after the old playground basketball game "Around the World." Team P is positioned in its first serve-receive pattern. Team X, which serves, is positioned in its base defensive position. Team X serves the ball to begin the drill, and Team P attempts to side out. If Team P comes up with the side out, it gets to rotate to its second serve-receive pattern, where it receives another serve from Team X.

Team P continues to rotate to the next serve-receive pattern, as long as it continues to side out. If Team P fails to side out, it can "chance it," and receive another serve from Team X. If Team P does not side out on the "chance," it must go back to its first serve-receive formation and serve to Team X. Team X then attempts to side out and rotate through all six serve-receive patterns.

The first team to rotate through all six serve-receive patterns is declared the winner. If a team chooses not to chance it, that team must stay in its rotation and serve and play defense until it has an opportunity to receive serve again. From that particular formation, the team's goal is to side out in the sixth pattern before the other team can do so.

Coaching Points: This drill enables the coach to evaluate the strengths and weaknesses of each serve-receive pattern.

Variations: Require the teams to side out twice before rotating. Dictate which play the teams must run in order to score a side out for rotation.

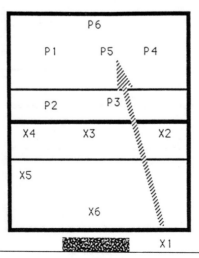

DRILL #92: TIP TRANSITION

Objective: To enhance team ball control while handling off-speed shots; to improve the ability to make perfect passes to the setter.

Setup: 12 players; 1 volleyball.

Description: The coach sets up two teams of six players, one team on each side of the court. The teams may start the drill in serve-receive formation or in their defensive position. The coach puts the ball in play with a free ball to one of the teams.

In this drill, the teams will attack each other only with off-speed shots or tips. The goal of both teams is to make perfect passes to the setter so that the setter can set any of three options on every play. Each team is working together to attempt to play the ball over the net a set amount of times (10–15) before rotating to the next formation. The coach counts out loud the number of times the ball passes over the net and, at the same time, judges the pass. If the pass is not to the setter's zone, the coach will stop the drill and start over, because the pass was not "good enough." Since the scoring must be continuous, the coach will start the count over again.

Coaching Points: The coach dictates the difficulty of this drill by being either a hard grader or an easy grader of passes. For players at lower skill levels, a good pass might be one that is passed in front of the attack line. For players at higher skill levels, the perfect pass would be to net zone 7—a pass that would not force the setter to move.

Variations: To work on serve-receive passing, as well as ball control, start the drill with a serve.

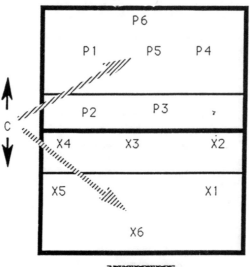

DRILL #93: THIRTEEN-ZERO BLOCKING

Objective: To promote better concentration when blocking; to promote blocking with a purpose.

Setup: 12 players; 1 volleyball.

Description: Set up a six-on-six situation, with the serving team leading, 13-0, and holding serve throughout the drill. Use rally scoring; however, keep in mind that the only way the serving team may score is with a stuff block. The receiving team, on the other hand, may score any way possible.

Coaching Points: Since the serving team cannot score (except in rare instances), the receiving team may find the tip to be a valuable weapon. To offset this conservative approach, however, the coach can award a point to the serving team if it is able to pick up the tip and convert it on the first swing. This drill forces the players to focus on blocking with the intent of stuff blocking.

Variation: Allow the serving team to score half a point for every ball it blocks back into its opponent's court.

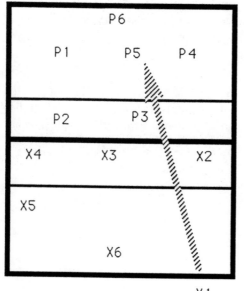

DRILL #94: FREE-BALL OFFENSE

Objective: To enhance the ability to handle free balls with the determination to put every one of them away.

Setup: 12 players; a steady supply of volleyballs.

Description: The coach sets up a six-on-six scrimmage situation and starts the drill by throwing a free ball over the net and into one of the courts. From that point, the scoring team will always receive the free ball from the coach. Only the team that receives a free ball can score a point on that particular rally. As long as the team either continues to put free balls away or wins the rally, it continues to score points and also continues to receive the free ball for the opportunity to score another point. If the team that doesn't receive the free ball wins the rally, then it has stopped the other team's run and will get the next free ball, and, of course, the opportunity to score. The winner is the first team to reach 30 points.

After the game ends, both teams rotate, and the second game starts with a score of 0-0. This process should be repeated for all six rotation. If the score of the game is tied at 3 after six games have been played, each team must choose its one rotation for the tie-breaker.

Coaching Points: When scrimmaging your first team versus a team of subs, require your starters to play to 30 points, and your nonstarters to play to only 20 points.

Variations: The coach chooses the rotations to be used for the tie-breaker. In the tie-breaker, have the teams rotate each time before they receive the free ball. In order to shorten the game, allow the teams to score only when they put the ball away on the first swing, and when winning the rally would only give another free ball.

DRILL #95: SECOND CONTACT

Objective: To help your non-setters develop the proper technique for setting high-outside sets; to improve your defensive players' ability to defend against limited attack options.

Setup: 12 players; a steady supply of volleyballs.

Description: The coach sets up a six-on-six scrimmage situation and tells the players that only high-outside sets may be utilized. C1 begins the drill by tossing the ball to one side of the court; this toss represents the first contact. The ball continues in play until it is terminated.

At this juncture, a point is awarded. C2 tosses the next ball to the opposite side of the court, and the drill continues. The first team to 15 in rally scoring is declared the winner. The players should then rotate and play another game to 15, and continue in this manner for all six rotations. If the game is tied at 3 after six games, the teams should play one game (the tie-breaker), making sure to rotate after every point.

Coaching Points: Every player should be accountable for getting a good swing at the ball on every possession. The coach should give feedback on the specific skill of overhead passing and its possible effect on play.

Variation: Utilize this drill to train RF players to set, by tossing every first contact to the player in that position.

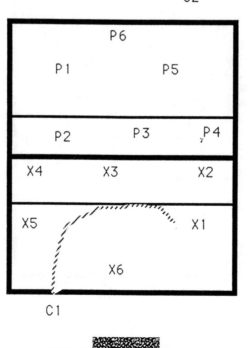

DRILL #96: BONGO

Setup: 12 players; a steady supply of volleyballs.

Objective: To solidify team defense; to improve transition offense.

Description: The coach sets up a six-on-six scrimmage situation and sends five balls to Team 1. The first ball is hit to the LB; the second, to the MB; and the third, to the RB. The fourth ball is a pursuit ball that is thrown anywhere in the gym, but on the pursuing team's side. The fifth ball is a served ball from Team 2.

In order to score a point, Team 1 must win five straight rallies (three from digs, one from a pursuit, and one from a serve-receive offense). If Team 1 does not win a rally, then Team 2 gets a turn (e.g., if Team 1 wins the first three rallies, but loses on the pursuit ball, then Team 2 gets a turn). Team 2 rotates before receiving the first ball, and then must win all five rallies in order to score a point. If Team 2 fails to complete its sequence of five victorious rallies, Team 1 rotates and gets another turn. Three total points wins the Bongo game.

Variation: In order to work on one-on-one blocking, the coach can choose to make this a five-on-five drill, eliminating the MB. This variation should make the scoring easier (a total of five points wins the game).

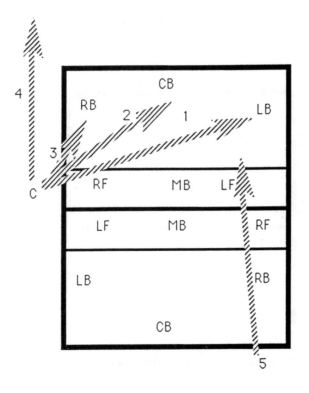

DRILL #97: FIRST SWING FOR POINTS

Objective: To stress the importance of putting the ball away on the first opportunity.

Setup: 12 players; 1 volleyball.

Description: The coach sets up a six-on-six scrimmage situation. Team P begins the drill by serving to Team X. If Team X is able to side out on its first swing, it scores a point. If Team X is denied a side-out on its first swing, and Team P is able to attack back and score on its first swing, then Team P scores a point. If neither team is able to score with its first swing, the rally continues to completion.

At this point, the serve goes to the team that has earned it; however, no points are awarded. The only other way to score a point is by a service ace. The remainder of the game is played in the traditional manner.

Coaching Points: This drill emphasizes the importance of the first swing and also encourages intense serving. It is important to always credit the ace serve with a point.

Variation: Play the same simulated game, but require that a score be credited only on the first side-out swing and an ace. This adjustment will lengthen the game, but it will also ensure that the players stay intense throughout.

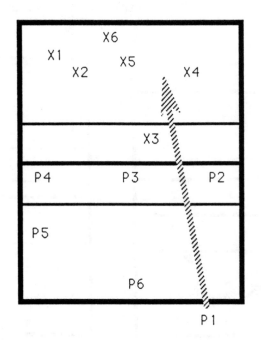

DRILL #98: BAM THROUGH THE BLOCK SIX-ON-SIX

Objective: To develop the ability to cover the hitter and attack repeatedly; to enhance the ability of the blockers to put up a solid, closed block.

Setup: 12 players; a steady supply of volleyballs.

Description: The coach sets up a six-on-six scrimmage situation and begins the drill by tossing a ball to either Team A or the hitting team. The setter sets the LF hitter, who has been instructed to "bam through the block." The team can score only if it bams the ball through the block or scores off the block or down the line or in the seam. The offensive team gets half a point every time it successfully covers the hitter and converts to another attack ball. The offensive team must score six full points before it can rotate.

If the coach is attempting to train both teams, he or she can toss the ball to the other team at this point. This drill should be worked on from both the serve-receive and defensive positions.

Coaching Points: This drill is designed to promote hitter coverage and good blocking technique; blockers rarely get to evaluate their block, because hitters hit around the block. Another plus of this drill is that it helps hitters learn to use a block and hit the seam (not just around the block to where the defenders are positioned).

Variations: Run the same drill for the MF and RF hitters, so that they can practice covering those positions. This drill, which can also be started with a serve, makes it possible to cover every variation of serve-receive plays.

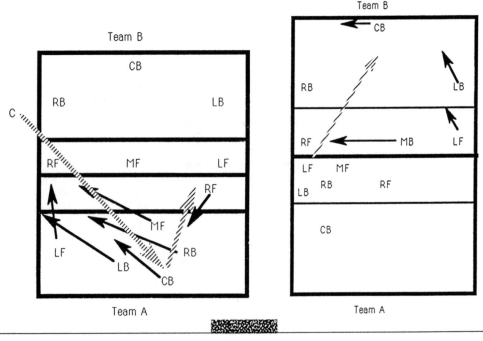

124

DRILL #99: BASEBALL/SOFTBALL

Objective: To place the team in a competitive situation that allows repetition in each rotation.

Setup: 12 players; 1 volleyball.

Description: The coach sets up a six-on-six scrimmage situation and designates the serving team as either the offensive or defensive team. Play proceeds, with the following rules in effect.

In the first scenario, the serving team is the offensive team. Play six innings (or the same number of innings as players on the team) and serve only one time through. The server gets three outs. A server error is an out. A service ace is a home run. Anytime the serving team scores a point, it is a base hit (four base hits equals a run). Anytime the receiving team earns what should be a side-out, it is an out. No limitations are placed on the number of runs that can be scored in any one inning. Any illegal hit is either an out or a base hit. Once the server makes three outs, the defensive team becomes the offensive team.

In the second scenario, the serving team is the defensive team. Play six innings (or the same number of innings as players on the team) and serve only one time through. The server (pitcher) gets to serve three outs. Service errors constitute a hit batter (one base). A service ace is an out. For the offensive team to get on base and score, it must put a ball away. The number of times the ball is taken over the net before it is put away will determine how many bases are awarded: first time is a home run; second time is a triple; third time is a double; fourth time is a single; fifth time is either a foul ball or an out. Anytime the defensive (serving) team puts the ball away, it is an out. Any illegal contact results in an error and either a runner on first or an out. The players move up on the bases according to the type of hit (i.e., single equals one base, double equals two bases, etc.).

Coaching Points: This drill provides an interesting way for the team to scrimmage and also work on offense and defense in each of the six rotations.

Variations: This drill can be modified in many ways by eliminating certain rules. Also, if the coach wants to work on certain aspects of the game, those aspects can be built into the rules (e.g., only if the MH puts the ball down is it an out or a hit; only a stuff block counts as an out or a hit; the outside hitters must hit line for an out or a hit).

DRILL #100: WASH

Objective: To promote persistence and competitiveness; to help the coach evaluate the strengths and weaknesses of every offensive and defensive formation.

Setup: 12 players; a steady supply of volleyballs.

Description: The coach sets up a six-on-six scrimmage situation. In this drill, a team must score two whole points before it either rotates or earns the serve. A team scores half a point for every ball it puts away. The serving team starts the drill with a serve. The receiving team attempts to side out. Regardless of the outcome of that attempt, the serving team immediately receives a free ball from the coach and attempts to win the rally. If the serving team wins both the serve and the free-ball rally, it has earned one big point. If the receiving team wins both rallies, it also earns one big point. If both teams win one of the rallies, then a "wash" is called, and no point is awarded. The server continues to serve until one team earns two big points. If the serving team wins two big points, it earns the right to rotate and receive the serve. The new serving team must stay in its first rotation and now serve. If the first receiving team scores two big points, it also earns the right to rotate and serve. The first serving team must stay in the same rotation until it has scored two big points while serving from that formation. The first team that makes it through all six rotations wins. (Note: Each team must serve and receive in each rotation.)

Coaching Points: This drill forces teams to practice longer in the weaker rotations and also allows the coach the opportunity to study and correct through repetition.

Variations: This drill can be cut shorter by requiring only one big point before rotation. The coach can also specify that only certain attacks will count for points (e.g., to work on MH transition, only the middle attacks score points). If the teams are not balanced, require the first team to score two big points, and the second team to score one big point. If there is a big drop-off in skill level between the first and second scrimmage teams, have the second team stay in the same position and not rotate throughout the drill.

DRILL #101: THE WAVE

Objective: To end practice with a fun, competitive drill, so that players and coaches look forward to coming back the next day.

Setup: 12–18 players; 4–6 volleyballs.

Description: The coach instructs the players to line up on the baseline by position (e.g., right-side players at RB, middles at CB, left-side players at LB). The first three players in each line become a team and position themselves in the backcourt on the far side of the net. The second players in line take the frontcourt, on the far side of the court (This is the valued position). The third players in each line take the frontcourt, on the near side of the court. The fourth players in each line position themselves in the backcourt, on the near side. The remaining players in line comprise Teams 5 and 6, and they wait to enter the court.

The teams of three work together throughout this drill. The goal of each team is to be positioned in the far frontcourt for as many rallies as possible (This is the earned and valued position, and the team can score only from this position).

Every rally won in this position counts as one point. The coach will either designate how many points win the game or let the players decide the winning number. The RF player is the setter for her team of three. The ball is put in play with a free ball from the coach to the near side, and the rally is played out. If the rally is won by the near side, the coach calls, "Wave," and the teams rotate forward throughout the drill, and no point is scored. Team 1 in the backcourt chases the ball and returns to the end of the line.

If the far side wins the rally, the coach calls "Flip-flop," and the nearside front court and the farside backcourt trade places. The farside front-court team (Team 2) is awarded one point, and the drill continues. When a team scores, no new teams enter the court.

The same four teams play out the next rally, although two teams are now in different positions. The ball is put in play again by the coach, to the nearside backcourt. (The diagrams below depict the teams by number and show the starting positions, as well as the switches made when both a wave and a flip-flop occur.

Coaching Points: This is a great end-of-practice drill. Since the teams do not always have equal numbers of players who play different positions, some players are forced to play out of position (e.g., a defensive specialist plays MB), which adds the ingredient of fun for them. The coach should remind non-setters to set off the net so that they avoid injury at the net on sets that are too tight. The coach could even instruct the players to stop on tight sets so that a replay will be called.

Variation: When 12 players are used, the drill is run without teams having to wait.

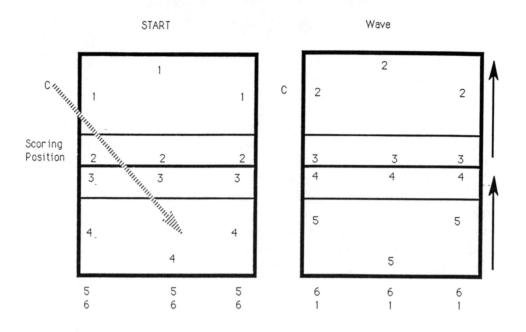

START

Wave

C

Scoring
Position

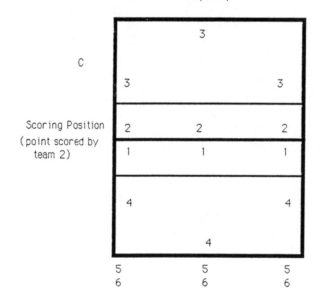

Flip/Flop

C

Scoring Position
(point scored by
team 2)

AUTHOR

One of the most highly respected and successful coaches in the country, Peggy Martin has guided Central Missouri State's program for 22 years with unprecedented success. Her teams have won 16 consecutive Mid-America Intercollegiate Athletics Association championships and made 15 consecutive appearances in the NCAA Division II Tournament. With 751 career victories, Martin is the winningest coach in Division II and only one of 11 college coaches, regardless of division, to reach the 700-win plateau. Martin's career record at Central Missouri is 751-191-8, for a winning percentage of .797. She has taken the Jennies to the Division II Elite Eight six times, finishing second in 1987 and fourth in 1994, 1995, and 1996. For the past four years, she has been chair of the NCAA Division II Volleyball Committee.

Martin has been chosen MIAA or (prior to 1982) Missouri AIAW Coach of the Year 13 times and AVCA South Central Regional Coach of the Year six times. In 1987, she was selected AVCA Division II Coach of the Year for guiding the Jennies to a 42-4 record and a runner-up finish at the national tournament.

Martin came to Central Missouri State in 1975 from Florida Southern College, where she had coached the volleyball and softball programs on the club level for one season. In addition to her 22 years as the Jennies' volleyball coach, Martin was also head softball coach from 1975 to 1987 compiling a 175-156 record and winning two MIAA championships. She served as assistant women's basketball coach at Central Missouri in 1976–77, as well as assistant athletic director from 1986 to 1988.

A native of Mobile, Alabama, Martin received her bachelor's degree in 1972 from Indiana University, where she lettered in basketball, softball and field hockey. She completed work on her master's degree in 1974 at the University of North Carolina–Greensboro and earned her doctorate in 1980 from Indiana University.